FOUNDATIONS OF MODERN PSYCHOLOGY SERIES

Richard S. Lazarus, *Editor*

THE PSYCHOLOGICAL DEVELOPMENT OF THE CHILD, Paul H. Mussen

TESTS AND MEASUREMENTS, Leona E. Tyler

MOTIVATION AND EMOTION, Edward J. Murray

PERSONALITY AND ADJUSTMENT, Richard S. Lazarus

CLINICAL PSYCHOLOGY, Julian B. Rotter

SENSORY PSYCHOLOGY, Conrad G. Mueller

PERCEPTION, Julian E. Hochberg

LEARNING, Sarnoff A. Mednick

LANGUAGE AND THOUGHT, John B. Carroll

SOCIAL PSYCHOLOGY, William W. Lambert and Wallace E. Lambert

PHYSIOLOGICAL PSYCHOLOGY, Philip Teitelbaum

EDUCATIONAL PSYCHOLOGY, Donald R. Green

THE NATURE OF PSYCHOLOGICAL INQUIRY, Ray Hyman

ORGANIZATIONAL PSYCHOLOGY, Edgar H. Schein

The Psychological Development of the Child

PAUL H. MUSSEN

Professor of Psychology and Research Psychologist in the Institute of Human Development, University of California, Berkeley; author and editor of books and journal articles in developmental psychology and research methods in child development; associate editor of several pyschological journals.

The Psychological Development of the Child

PRENTICE-HALL, INC., *Englewood Cliffs, New Jersey*

Printed in the United States of America. Library of Congress Catalog Card No.: 63–18023

THE PSYCHOLOGICAL DEVELOPMENT OF THE CHILD, *Paul H. Mussen*

PRENTICE-HALL FOUNDATIONS OF MODERN PSYCHOLOGY SERIES

Richard S. Lazarus, *Editor*

Current printing (last digit):

15 14 13 12 11 10 9

Designed by Harry Rinehart

C–73227(p), C–73228(c)

TO ETHEL, MICHELE, AND JIMMY

Foundations of Modern Psychology Series

The tremendous growth and vitality of psychology and its increasing fusion with the social and biological sciences demand a new approach to teaching at the introductory level. The basic course, geared as it usually is to a single text that tries to skim everything—that sacrifices depth for superficial breadth—is no longer adequate. Psychology has become too diverse for any one man, or a few men, to write about with complete authority. The alternative, a book that ignores many essential areas in order to present more comprehensively and effectively a particular aspect or view of psychology, is also insufficient. For in this solution, many key areas are simply not communicated to the student at all.

The Foundations of Modern Psychology is a new and different approach to the introductory course. The instructor is offered a series of short volumes, each a self-contained book on the special issues, methods, and content of a basic topic by a noted authority who is actively contributing to that particular field. And taken together, the volumes cover the full scope of psychological thought, research, and application.

The result is a series that offers the advantage of tremendous flexibility and scope. The teacher can choose the subjects he wants to emphasize and present them in the order he desires. And without necessarily sacrificing breadth, he can provide the student with a much fuller treatment of individual areas at the introductory level than is normally possible. If he does not have time to include all the volumes in his course, he can recommend the omitted ones as outside reading, thus covering the full range of psychological topics.

Psychologists are becoming increasingly aware of the importance of reaching the introductory student with high-quality, well-written, and stimulating material, material that highlights the continuing and exciting search for new knowledge. The Foundations of Modern Psychology Series is our attempt to place in the hands of instructors the best textbook tools for this purpose.

Preface

No volume as brief as this could possibly present a complete or exhaustive survey of the principles, facts, and theories of child development. This is in no sense a condensed or simplified textbook of child psychology. Rather, the book is designed to give the reader with little or no training in the field a broad perspective of its objectives, scope, and contents.

As a discipline, child development is concerned with the description and explanation—the *hows* and *whys*—of human growth and change. Its data and theories are derived from, and contribute to, many disciplines: among them, psychology (particularly the areas of perception, learning, social behavior, and personality), physiology, sociology, anthropology, and pediatrics.

The focal points of this book are the basic ideas, problems, and issues with which researchers and theorists, as well as people working with children, have been concerned. In discussing these, I have attempted to stress the interrelationships among the contributing disciplines and to present major concepts and theories of child development, together with a representative sample of well-established, scientifically valid, empirical findings. The emphasis throughout is on contemporary thought and research.

But facts and theories alone do not provide an adequate basis for understanding child development as a scientific discipline. This requires some knowledge of the methods of the field—of how facts are discovered. Hence, considerable attention is given to the research design and to observational, experimental, and testing techniques used in investigating developmental phenomena. Familiarity with these methods may help the student to read more critically and wisely both the professional literature and the abundant popular works on child development and child rearing.

Hopefully, an understanding of how research in this field is conducted, plus some mastery of the inherently fascinating subject matter—which is merely *sampled* in this small book—will stimulate some students to pursue further their attempts to explore systematically the intricacies of human development.

Paul H. Mussen

Contents

The Psychological Development of the Child

The Field of Child Psychology

"Rich man, poor man, beggar man, thief, doctor, lawyer, Indian chief . . ." Which will Johnny, age three days, become? If he's not an Indian, he can't be an Indian chief, but he might achieve any of the other positions mentioned in the children's refrain.

What are the factors that determine what an individual becomes—what forces shape his abilities, interests, motives, goals, desires, personality characteristics, and social attitudes? In short, how does he develop into the kind of person he becomes? The question is very broad, but, in a sense, it summarizes the basic issues of the field of child psychology.

1

As a scientific discipline, child psychology is less than a century old. But even centuries ago, some of the problems of the field, which are now investigated by systematic research, were the subjects of discussion and literary essay. Many prominent classical philosophers thought and wrote about the characteristics of children and the factors affecting their development. Plato recognized that, to some extent, individual differences in ability are inborn, but he also realized that early childhood training and teaching help to determine later vocational choice and adjustment. The English philosopher John Locke also believed that early discipline fostered the development of the self-discipline and self-control he considered the cardinal adult virtues. Jean-Jacques Rousseau, the French philosopher, also thought that the experiences of the first few years are crucial in a person's development. In contrast to Locke, however, he advocated that children be allowed free expression of their "natural impulses," which, according to his beliefs, are inherently noble and just.

These and other philosophers thought and wrote about problems that still concern the child psychologist. But the psychologist does not simply speculate about those problems. Rather, he seeks systematic, scientific solutions to them.

THE GOALS OF CHILD PSYCHOLOGY

What, then, are the goals and objectives of modern scientific child psychology? Fundamentally there are two broad, interlocking aims. The first goal, simply stated, is to *describe,* as completely and precisely as possible, children's psychological functions at different ages and to discover the characteristics of changes in those functions with age. The second, more recently developed goal is to *explain* age changes in behavior—to discover the processes underlying these changes.

Traditionally, research in child psychology, even to the present day, has focused on the first problem: the nature and rates of change in various aspects of behavior—for example, sensory and motor ability, perception and intellectual functions, social and emotional reactions. In fact, most of our current knowledge of child psychology concerns age trends in development.

The earliest recorded systematic observations of child development, the so-called "baby biographies," appeared in the late eighteenth and nineteenth centuries. Typically, these were accounts of the development of one child (usually the author's own child, niece, or nephew) that attempted to trace changes in sensory, motor, language, and intellectual capacity. These works were biased and based on selective observation, hence they cannot be considered scientific. But they did excite a great deal of interest in the study of children and they pointed out some of the major problems of child psychology.

Toward the end of the nineteenth century, G. Stanley Hall of Clark University began to investigate systematically what he referred to as "the contents of children's minds." He administered questionnaires—series of questions that could be answered in writing—to large groups of children. These were designed to gather information about the behavior, attitudes, and interests of children and adolescents. Hall's purpose, like that of the baby biographers, was to describe accurately the nature of the "contents of the minds"—thoughts, feelings, and emotions—of children of different ages, and to determine age trends, that is, to trace how these functions change as children grow older.

As interest in the field of child psychology increased, psychologists devised better methods and collected better data on various aspects of development. For example, careful, objective studies have established the exact nature and sequence of the development of motor activities such as grasping, block-building, and locomotion (sitting and walking). We also have fairly accurate knowledge of language development from the earliest utterances of unrefined, infantile sounds to communication in complex, grammatically correct sentences. Later in this volume we shall review some excellent research that traces in detail the stages of intellectual development from infant perception to adult reasoning ability. These are merely a few examples of the many psychological functions whose developmental courses have been described.

Age trend data are important for several reasons. Such information may be useful in formulating general principles of development. Moreover, these data provide *averages* or *norms* of various aspects of development that can be used in evaluating the status of individual children. Is this particular child below or above average in height? Is his vocabulary large, small, or average for his age? Judging from his interactions with other children, is he socially mature or immature? Standards or norms derived from age trend research may also be useful in diagnosing problems of physical or psychological development.

Although the description of age trends has traditionally been the predominant concern of child psychology, recent research in the field has largely been centered on the second goal, the explanation of the observed age trends. *Why* does the child become less awkward and more agile in walking, more fluent in talking, and better at solving complex problems as he grows older? To what extent are these changes due to "nature"—built-in biological characteristics of the human organism, genetic factors, or maturation of the nervous system? And to what extent are they determined, or strongly influenced, by "nurture"—learning or stimulation of the environment?

The study of individual variations among children is closely related to this second problem. Children not only change with age, but at any given age, they also show marked individual differences in many aspects of development. If you observe a group of normal four-year-olds in a nursery school, you will find some who talk like adults, and some who have meager vocabularies and are infantile in their speech habits, pronunciation, and grammar. Investigation of such individual differences may contribute to an understanding of the determinants of general age changes in language development. For example, if children who are advanced in speech at this age are found to differ genetically from those who are relatively retarded, you may infer that rate of change in language facility is dependent on heredity. If, on the other hand, investigation reveals that children advanced in speech receive more encouragement for verbal accomplishment and practice speaking more than others, you may infer that improvements with age in language ability are attributable, at least in part, to increased speech practice and stimulation.

As we shall stress repeatedly throughout this volume, the answers to questions about the *hows* and *whys* of age changes and of individual differences are enormously complex.

Developmental phenomena must often be explained in terms of the knowledge accumulated in many different content areas: learning, perception, motivation, social psychology, the psychology of personality, genetics, physiology, anthropology, sociology. The research developmental psychologist is primarily interested in pure research, in extending—but not necessarily applying—scientific knowledge. Nevertheless, the findings of his research may be applied in many fields, such as pediatrics, psychiatry, social work, educational psychology, counseling and guidance, special education, and therapeutic work with handicapped children such as the blind, deaf, retarded, and disturbed. The experiences of professional workers in these disciplines may be rich sources of information about psychological development and of suggestions of problems in need of further research.

Here are some examples of the interrelationships among disciplines. Certain characteristics (such as physical appearance and growth rates), intelligence, and certain forms of mental deficiency and mental illness, are, at least partially, hereditarily determined; to understand these fully, the developmental psychologist needs some knowledge of genetics. The striking physical and behavioral changes of adolescence are strongly influenced by basic physiological processes involving the endocrine glands and the biochemistry of the blood system; in investigating these phenomena, the psychologist must draw upon findings in physiology and endocrinology. From research in pediatrics comes pertinent information on the influences of illnesses, malnutrition, and drugs on physical and psychological growth and change. Psychiatry has contributed many facts and theories about how early childhood events affect the behavior, adjustment, and maladjustment of older children, adolescents, and adults. Many of a person's motives, feelings, attitudes, and interests are strongly conditioned by the social group to which he belongs, whether social class, or minority, racial, or religious group; anthropology and sociology have provided extremely valuable data about the impacts of these elements of social structure on personality, social characteristics, and development. Clearly, a comprehensive understanding of developmental psychology, of age changes and the mechanisms or processes underlying them, involves the integration of many kinds of data drawn from many scientific disciplines.

Progress in the field of developmental psychology has been rapid and often exciting. Still, there are many areas in which our knowledge is very limited. For one example, there are a number of plausible theories about the effects of the early child-rearing practices of parents on a child's later personality, but scientific evidence bearing on these theories is incomplete. For another, the stages leading to the development of adult problem-solving ability have been described in detail, but we do not fully understand what accounts for the transitions from one stage to the next. There are many interesting, promising, and active programs of research on these and similar problems but, for many aspects of behavior, it is still difficult—and in some cases impossible—to describe developmental stages precisely, or to specify the determinants of change.

In evaluating the findings of developmental research, we must distinguish between *description* and *explanation*. Phenomena must be described before they can be explained, but description itself cannot give us any understanding of why the phenomena occur or of processes or determinants involved. For instance, the finding that two-year-olds tend to be more negativistic than three-year-olds is merely *descriptive;* it provides no information about the reasons underlying the two-year-old's negativism. It may be tempting to the student to explain a child's behavior in terms of his age alone ("He is negativistic because he is two years old"), but this is hardly a scientifically satisfactory statement.

In the present volume, we shall review some of the most important and well-established findings in child psychology. We shall discuss physical growth, sensory capacities, perception, intelligence, reasoning, personality and social behavior, giving our attention to age trends in development and to the factors underlying these trends. We shall *sample* major ideas, research techniques, and findings of the field in an attempt to present a general picture of what child psychologists do, how they work, and what they have discovered.

A word of caution about the presentation seems appropriate. For purposes of convenience in exposition and study, development may be broken down into a number of aspects, such as physical-biological, intellectual, personality, social, and so on. Actually, however, all aspects of development are continuous, concurrent, and closely and intricately interrelated. Developments in one area, directly or indirectly, affect developments in another. To cite some simple examples, while a child is changing in physical characteristics and appearance (probably, in large measure, as a result of heredity), his intelligence is increasing. His personality and social behavior also become modified. The latter changes are probably primarily a result of social experiences but, to some extent, they may also be influenced by increased intellectual ability and by rate of physical maturation. The child's personality clearly affects his relationships with others (that is, his social behavior), and even to some degree may affect intelligence and intellectual functions. In brief, aspects of development interact and affect one another; changes in one function are reflected in others. For this reason, isolating phases of the developmental process for purposes of discussion is admittedly arbitrary, and doing so gives a somewhat inaccurate picture. Therefore, the reader must constantly remind himself of the interrelatedness of *all* aspects of development.

THE METHODS OF CHILD PSYCHOLOGY

Before reviewing the *content* of child psychology, let us turn our attention briefly to the *methods* and *techniques* of research in this field. We cannot understand or evaluate the data of a scientific discipline without some understanding of how they were collected.

The developmental psychologist often uses broad methods of investigation and specific research techniques borrowed from other areas of psychology or from other disciplines. The research problem he is trying to solve will, of course, determine his choice of methods and instruments. The general method may be observational, experimental, or comparative, and the specific techniques may be derived from investigations in the fields of perception, physiological psychology, or the psychology of personality.

The fundamental method is, of course, careful, unbiased, observation of behavior. We may observe some phenomena, such as reactions to a peer group, or aggressiveness or sympathetic behavior, as they occur "naturally"—for example, in a nursery school or on a playground. We may make observations of other kinds of behavior under "standard" or "controlled" conditions, with the aid of mechanical devices that assure objectivity. For example, the study of trends in ability to grasp and manipulate objects would require careful and highly detailed observations of children of different ages, each manipulating the same object in a standard situation. To illustrate, we might individually "test" 40 children—ten each at the ages of 20 weeks, 30 weeks, 40 weeks, and 50 weeks—while they are sitting upright in a high chair. If we placed a block on a tray before each child, we would observe and record in detail his efforts to grasp and manipulate it. Motion picture records of the children's reactions would provide complete and objective records, which we could analyze carefully, noting the techniques of grasping (for instance, the use of arm, wrist, hand, and fingers). A comparison of the records of children of different ages would serve as the basis for describing age trends in the development of manipulative ability.

Whether he is making observations under "natural" or controlled conditions, an observer cannot observe *everything* about a child's behavior. Typically, he restricts his observations to some particular type of behavior. For example, in studying social development, a researcher may limit his attention specifically to aggression among children in nursery school, accurately recording all acts such as hitting, striking, quarreling, name-calling, or destroying another child's toys. Furthermore, since he cannot observe the children all the time, he is likely to use a time sampling approach, observing each child several times for specific short periods—say, five minutes on each of four occasions. If possible the researcher would *quantify*, or score, the expression of aggression.

Although behaviors such as manipulation and aggression are directly observable, many of the variables with which the child psychologist is concerned are not. Intelligence, personality characteristics, and basic motivations are not observable and must be inferred from behavior. To get at intelligence, for instance, a psychologist *observes* a child's performance of certain tasks and his solution of problems in carefully devised tests, and, from his observations, makes inferences about the child's intelligence level.

Such inferences can be valid and meaningful, however, only if the observations of behavior are made under standard or controlled conditions and if uniform procedures, identical for all subjects, are used. If the performances of different children are to be compared, the conditions under which they are observed must be the same for all. Then we can be sure that variations in the children's performance are due to variations in their intelligence level and not to other, extraneous variables. Suppose, for example, one child is tested in a noisy, stuffy room by a harsh or impolite examiner who presents him with difficult problems before giving him simple ones. Another child is tested by a kindly examiner in a quiet, pleasant room and solves problems in order of difficulty. Poorer performance by the first child might be due to his surroundings or the test procedure rather than to a lower level of intelligence. If the test circumstances were identical for the two subjects, however, we could more reasonably infer that the child who performed more poorly had less intelligence than the other.

Analogously, we may make inferences about relative strengths of children's aggressive motivations from observations of their fighting, arguing, and destructiveness. But, again, unless these observations are made under controlled, standard conditions, our inferences will probably not be valid. The amount of aggression a child displays varies with the nature of the situation as well as with the strength of his aggressive motivation. Hence we could learn very little about the relative basic aggressive motivations of two children if we observed one in a small, cluttered, overcrowded room and the other in a spacious, uncluttered, comfortable room.

The most highly preferred research method in child psychology, as in most scientific fields, is the *experiment*. This is also a method of controlled observation, but it is distinctive, for it always involves a controlled, prearranged *intervention* or *manipulation* by the experimenter. More specifically, the experimenter actually creates, controls, and manipulates *one* particular factor—called the independent variable—and then observes whether and how some other variable (or variables), the dependent one(s), changes as the independent one is manipulated. Only one factor is allowed to vary at a time; all others are held constant, that is, not allowed to vary.

To illustrate, suppose a psychological experimenter wants to test the effects of various degrees of frustration on the aggressive behavior of children. His hypothesis is that greater degrees of frustration lead to greater amounts of aggressive behavior. He could test this proposition experimentally with three groups of children, two experimental and one control. By equating the three groups in all characteristics in which he is not interested but which might affect aggressive expression (for example, age, grade placement, sex, health, intelligence, and socioeconomic class), the experimenter keeps these variables constant. He can then manipulate as he wishes the one variable in which he *is* interested, amount of frustration. He would, of course, subject the three groups to different degrees of frustration.

He might present the first group with a number of difficult or insoluble problems and require them to work at the tasks for a long time. The second group might be subjected to some milder frustration than the first, but for the same amount of time. The third group, the control, would engage in some kind of activity which would not produce any frustration at all. The experimenter might then place all three groups of children in a social situation in order to observe and record their aggressive behavior. He could then determine whether degree of frustration was, in fact, related to amount of aggression—that is, whether the group that had been subjected to the most frustration behaved most aggressively, and the control group the least so.

The unique and critical advantage of an experiment is that, since relevant factors are isolated, the precise effects of change in the independent variable on the dependent one can be demonstrated directly. Without experimental procedures, it is much more difficult to evaluate accurately the relative contributions of all the factors that may lead to a particular outcome or produce a particular effect. For example, the intensity of children's aggressive reactions to frustration would be affected by such factors as their sex, and social-class status, as well as by the experiences of frustration, presence or absence of adult authorities, and fear of punishment for aggression. Observational studies might yield some important data about the effects of these last variables, but these could be demonstrated and evaluated most clearly by experiments.

Unfortunately, there are many crucial problems in child psychology that cannot be solved by experimental studies. If, for example, an investigator wanted to determine precisely the effects on a child's personality development of parental attitudes such as rejection, he could hardly expect mothers to reject their children just so that he could perform an experiment. Still, he may be able, by means of interviews, to find mothers who have psychologically rejected their children and a comparable group of mothers who have accepted their children. If the children of the two groups of mothers were matched in age, intelligence, and socioeconomic status, comparison of the personality characteristics of the two groups of children would yield information on the effects of rejection.

If it is not possible to match the groups on all variables that might be related to the effects of rejection, sophisticated statistical techniques can sometimes be used to control or separate out the effects of some of them. A study in which variables other than the independent one are controlled by matching, or ruled out statistically—called variously "comparison of known groups," correlational study, or even a "field," or "natural," experiment—

cannot be considered an experiment, but it is as close an approximation as is possible under the circumstances.

One of the most exciting and fruitful recent trends in developmental psychology has been the application and extension of experimental approaches to many problems that were previously investigated exclusively by observational and correlational techniques. There have been experiments dealing with such complex variables as dependency, anxiety, guilt, language acquisition, problem solving, and concept formation. Moreover, many recent studies involve ingenious combinations of experimental and observational methods. Studies of this kind will be referred to at various times later in the book.

The specific research instruments used by child psychologists are drawn from, and are similar to, those used in other fields of psychology and in related disciplines. In studying physical growth, psychologists use *anthropometric* techniques developed by anatomists and physical anthropologists for measuring parts of the body and the maturity of the skeleton and various organs. They investigate developmental aspects of learning by methods, techniques, and apparatuses, adapted from research in adult learning (for example, lists of nonsense syllables). Research in intellectual growth and personality development involves the use of many kinds of techniques used in the study of adults, for example, intelligence tests, projective techniques,* and rating scales (completed, say, by teachers or camp counselors). Observational techniques, rating scales, and, wherever possible, experimental situations involving social interactions, are used in the study of social development.

In short, most of the research techniques of child psychology were not specifically designed for this field. There is, however, one general approach that is most characteristic of (although not unique to) this area. This is the *longitudinal method.* We can best explain this in contrast to the *cross-sectional method.* In the longitudinal approach, the same group of children is studied, tested, and observed repeatedly over an extended period of time. In investigating the development of reasoning ability and concept formation between the ages of four and ten longitudinally, a researcher would gather a group of subjects and give them appropriate tests, first when they were four years old, and, subsequently at annual or semiannual intervals until they were ten. Analysis of the results of his tests would permit him to define age trends in the development of these functions.

An investigator employing the cross-sectional method to study these developments would give these tests all at once to children of different ages, that is, to groups of four-year-olds, five-year-olds, six-year-olds, and so forth. Comparison of the performances of children of different ages would,

* Doll play is a projective technique specifically designed for work with children. A child is given dolls representing important people (mother, father, brother) and instructed to "make up a story" with them. It is assumed that, in his play, the child reveals his own deep feelings and emotions and his attitudes towards others.

as in the case of the longitudinal study, enable him to describe age trends in problem-solving and concept-formation ability. In short, age changes may be studied either by longitudinal or by cross-sectional methods.

There are several kinds of problems that can be adequately investigated only by means of the longitudinal method, however. For example, the study of *individual* trends in development must be longitudinal, for it requires repeated testing. We can determine whether personality, intelligence, or performance are stable, or consistent, over long periods of time only if we test the same individuals at different ages—a longitudinal approach. And we can most adequately evaluate latent, or delayed, effects of early experiences, such as parental overprotection, on later personality by longitudinal means—that is, by relating observations of early treatment to personality data collected later in the child's life.

Although it is very useful, the longitudinal method is extremely expensive and time-consuming, and it has some inherent limitations. For instance, we know little or nothing of how repeated exposure to psychological testing and observation affects the subjects in such studies, or of the possible biases investigators might develop as a result of their frequent contacts with the subjects. For these reasons, the method has not been widely used. The cross-sectional method has enjoyed far more frequent use in research in child psychology, so most of the data reported in this volume come from studies of this kind.

General Principles of Development

Development is a continuous process that begins when life does, at conception. This event occurs at the moment the egg in the mother is fertilized, its wall being penetrated by a sperm cell from the father. Immediately following conception, the process of *mitosis,* or cell division, is initiated. The fertilized ovum, a single cell, divides and subdivides rapidly, until millions of cells have been formed. As development proceeds, the new cells assume highly specialized functions, becoming parts of various body systems—nervous, skeletal, muscular, or circulatory. The fetus, as a child is called before it is born, begins to take shape.

2

The sequence of development in the prenatal (before birth) period is fixed and invariable. The head, eyes, trunk, arms, legs, genitals, and internal organs develop in the same order and at approximately the same prenatal ages in all fetuses. Just about nine months after conception, the child is born.

Several broad principles of development operate in both the prenatal and early postnatal periods. First, development is, for the most part, orderly and proceeds in an unvarying sequence. All fetuses can turn their heads before they can extend their hands. Postnatally, the baby grows and his motor abilities increase in a patterned way. Every child "sits before he stands . . . babbles before he talks . . . draws a circle before he draws a square . . . is dependent on others before he achieves dependence on self." *

Second, although development is continuous, it is not always smooth and gradual. There are spurts in physical growth and psychological functioning: abrupt increases in height, weight, and size of genital organs during early adolescence; sharp rises in vocabulary during the preschool years; sudden improvements in problem-solving abilities during adolescence.

Moreover, there are *critical periods* for the development of certain organs or functions; interference with normal development at such periods is likely to result in permanent deficiencies or malfunctions. For example, embryological research has shown that there are critical periods in the development of the fetus's organs (heart, eyes, kidneys). Erik Erikson, a psychoanalyst, has suggested that the first year of life is the critical period for the development of trust in others. The infant who does not receive adequate warmth and love during this time may fail to develop a sense of trust and, as a result, may remain permanently inadequate in social relationships. Analogously, there seem to be periods of "readiness" for learning various tasks, such as reading or bicycle riding. The child who does not learn these tasks during these periods may have great difficulty learning them later.

The experiences at one stage of maturity affect future developments. If an expectant mother contracts rubella (German measles), the child in her uterus may be born defective and remain so. Psychoanalysts and clinical psychologists have abundant evidence that a child who fails to develop self-confidence and trust early in life is likely to be emotionally unstable and maladjusted during adolescence.

DIRECTIONS OF DEVELOPMENT

Several basic directional trends of development have been delineated. One is the *cephalocaudal*, or head-to-foot, direction of development. As an illustration, a fetus's head is well developed before his legs assume their final form; arm buds appear before leg buds. After birth, the head region develops in advance of the lower parts of the body. Improvements in visual fixation

* Gesell, A. L., and Ilg, F. *Infant and child in the culture of today*. New York: Harpers, 1943.

and eye-hand coordination precede the effective use of arms and hands in reaching and grasping. A child achieves these abilities, in turn, before he can use his legs adequately in standing and walking.

Development also proceeds in a *proximodistal* or outward, direction, the central parts of the body maturing earlier and becoming functional before those toward the periphery. Thus, an infant exhibits gross arm and forearm movements before he moves his wrists, hands, and fingers. In reaching, he uses his shoulders and elbows effectively before he uses his wrist and fingers. In locomotion, the upper arm and upper leg are brought under voluntary control before the forearm, foreleg, hands, and feet.

Another general directional trend is from *mass* to *specific* activities, or from large to small muscles. Most of an infant's earliest reactions are mass, diffuse, and undifferentiated movements of the whole body or large segments of it. These crude, awkward early movements are gradually replaced by more refined, differentiated, precise, and effective reactions. Similarly, a child's initial attempts at grasping are gross and clumsy, compared with the refined thumb and forefinger movements he will make a few months later. His first steps, too, are accompanied by many awkward excess movements that decrease gradually until he uses only appropriate muscles and limbs in walking.

The Russian psychologists, beginning with Ivan Pavlov, have pointed out some important age trends in the nature of a child's orientation, and attention, to the world around him. They refer to the orienting, or "what is it," reflex, which is the infant's first response to stimuli that are unexpected and unfamiliar. The earliest orienting reflexes, ready at birth, are gross movements such as postural changes in response to being held upright or falling, and the head movements involved in seeking the mother's breast or the nipple of a bottle. Between two and five weeks, the infant begins to move his eyes and head in response to sound and visual stimuli. These are somewhat passive, primitive investigatory responses, but with further elaboration, elimination of excess movements, greater precision and streamlining, they seem to be used more actively, being manifested in relation to every new stimulus. The child develops an exploratory attitude toward the environment, turning his head to a voice at six months, and searching for, and grasping, objects in order to investigate them and to orient himself. Orienting reflexes become less frequent in well-defined and familiar situations as the child grows older, but from these early responses emerge tendencies toward curiosity and exploration of new situations.

MATURATION AND LEARNING

All the characteristics and abilities a person acquires and all developmental changes result from two basic, though complex, processes: learning and maturation. Since the two processes almost always interact, it is difficult to separate their effects from each other or to specify the relative contribution of each to a child's development. Clearly, growth in height is not learned but depends on maturation, a biological process. But improvements in motor activities, such as walking, depend on maturation *and* learning, and the interaction between them.

What, then, are maturation and learning? Developmental psychologists are not entirely in agreement, though there is a common core of accepted meaning. Thus all definitions of *maturation* stress *organic processes or structural changes occurring within an individual's body that are relatively independent of external environmental conditions, experiences, or practice.* "*By 'maturation' is meant development of the organism as a function of time, or age;* maturation refers to neurophysiological-biochemical changes from conception to death." *

Learning has also been defined in diverse ways, but the term generally refers to changes in behavior or performance as a consequence of experience. Ernest R. Hilgard, an outstanding learning theorist, speaks of learning as "the process by which an activity originates or is changed through training procedures (whether in the laboratory or in the natural environment) as distinguished from changes not attributable to training." †

A number of important and stimulating theories of learning have been proposed, each with its own set of principles and hypotheses for explaining the learning process. For our purposes, we do not need to be concerned with the specific details of the learning process, even though learning plays a crucial—probably, indeed, the most important—role in most aspects of development and change. We shall employ only a few generally accepted principles of learning in this volume.

Specifically, we accept the principle that a child will learn a response more effectively and more thoroughly if he is *motivated*—that is, if he has some need or desire—to learn it. Moreover, he will learn a response better if he is *reinforced,* or *rewarded,* for learning it—that is, if the learning leads to the satisfaction of some of his needs. According to this view, the more a response is rewarded, the stronger it becomes and the more likely it is to be repeated. Although in the author's opinion most learning does involve motivation and reward, it has been demonstrated that some learning occurs without them.

The interactions between maturation and learning processes are particularly clear in motor development—especially postural responses, locomotion, and manipulation—which we shall discuss in greater detail in Chapter 3. Boyd McCandless, a prominent child psychologist, has provided an excellent statement that clarifies the interrelationships between the two processes and illustrates the principle that *maturation is essential to learning*.

Increased height, weight, and strength, then, are in part the result of maturation (time and nutrition). But organizing these maturational phenomena so that per-

* McCandless, B. R. *Children and adolescents—behavior and development*. New York: Holt, Rinehart and Winston, 1961, p. 118.

† Hilgard, E. R. *Theories of learning*. New York: Appleton-Century-Crofts, 1948, p. 4.

formances previously impossible for the child can be accomplished involves *learning*. A baby sits alone (at about 6 months of age) in part because he has grown or matured. His head, in proportion to his torso and legs, is smaller; his back muscles, in consequence of both maturation and exercise, are stronger. As he has grown, he has practiced constantly. He has reared up from his stomach, using his arms as props; he has practiced balancing his head, he has used his legs. While lying on his back, he has tried to pull himself up by his hands and arms. Presently, he puts these separate learned skills together; and a new behavior, the effect partly of learning, partly of maturation, results; he sits up alone.*

* McCandless, B. R. *Ibid.,* p. 118.

3 Biological Bases of Development

Until a child is born, his development is influenced primarily by biologically determined forces of maturation. Hence, careful study of neonates (newborn children) can shed light on the problem of which needs, sensory capacities, and motor abilities are inborn and so independent of learning and environmental stimulation. In addition, many new motor and sensory functions and abilities emerge very soon after birth without special training or stimulation, apparently largely as a function of maturation. A neonate's needs, sensory capacities, and response capabilities constitute the bases on which a great deal of subsequent learning and behavior is built.

Physical Characteristics of Neonates

Before surveying these innate qualities, however, let us look briefly at a neonate's general physical state. His body grows extremely rapidly during the first year, relative increases in size and weight being greater than at any later time. The baby's birth weight—about seven pounds on the average for boys and slightly less for girls—doubles during the first six months and almost triples in the first year. Body length, for boys about 20 inches at birth on the average, increases over one third, to about 28 or 29 inches by the end of the first year.

During infancy, different parts of the body grow at different rates until body proportions become more like an adult's. In accordance with the head-to-foot principle of development, the head and upper parts of the body grow at a faster pace than the trunk and legs. Head size increases at an amazing rate, beginning almost immediately after conception, and by birth, the head is about 60 per cent as large as it will be in adulthood. A newborn baby appears to be top heavy, the length of his head being one quarter of his total body length. The brain doubles in size during the first two years.

The trunk ranks second to the head in over-all growth rate, reaching approximately 50 per cent of its full (adult) length by the end of the second year. Of all the parts of the neonate's body, his legs are furthest from adult size, and, relative to the upper parts of the body, they grow slowly.

Neonates' Needs

Many of the important needs or motives of older children and adults are *learned* as a result of social experience and environmental stimulation. For example, the needs for love from the mother, for social status, and for achievement of financial success are not innate, but *learned needs.*

Several basic biological needs of human beings are innate, however. These include the needs for oxygen, for elimination, for food and drink, for temperature regulation. An individual's survival depends on the satisfaction of these needs. In infancy, many needs are gratified in a self-regulatory manner, without voluntary control or active participation by the infant or by others. For example, reflex breathing mechanisms provide a neonate with enough oxygen to take care of his requirements. Reflexive sphincter action takes care of his need for elimination, and, under ordinary circumstances and within certain limits, automatic physiological reactions keep his body at a relatively constant temperature. His body's chemical and physiological balances, and thus his energy, are maintained through sleep. Unless the infant is ill, in pain, or extremely uncomfortable, he will sleep as much as he needs to and awaken when he is rested. On the average, for the first few weeks of their lives, infants spend about 80 per cent of their time asleep, although there are vast individual differences.

Of a neonate's basic biological needs, two, hunger and thirst, are not satisfied automatically. Gratification of these needs requires help from someone else and if this is not given promptly, an infant's tensions may become intense and painful. The social relationships involved in the satisfaction of these needs are among the infant's most important early experiences, and may have enduring effects on personality development (see Chapter 5).

Sensory Abilities

If an infant is to learn from the environment, he must "notice" its salient characteristics; that is, he must be able to see, hear, smell, touch, and feel. The neonate's sensory capacities have been studied carefully, but many important developmental questions are still unanswered. A few facts have been clearly established, however. Sense by sense, they are as follows:

The structure, neuromuscular apparatus, and functioning of the eyes are not perfected at birth, but they improve very rapidly. Coordination and convergence of the eyes, required for visual fixation and depth perception, begin to develop immediately after birth and appear to be fairly well established by the age of seven or eight weeks. Infants as young as 15 days of age can discriminate differences in brightness and hue. Swing a bright gold object before him, or project a moving colored spot on the ceiling above, and a baby will follow it with his eyes. When presented with a pair of stimuli—one complex (such as a checkerboard or bull's eye) and one simple (a circle or a square)—infants two weeks old prefer to gaze at the more complex pattern.

If a tone is sounded in his presence and then made louder or softer, a neonate may respond strongly—for example, with changes in gross body movements and in heart and breathing rates. This reaction indicates that neonates hear differences in loudness. They do not appear to be sensitive to differences in pitch, however.

So far as can be determined, neonates are sensitive only to markedly pleasant or unpleasant odors, but reactions to differences in taste (sucking in response to sweet-tasting substances and grimacing to sour ones) appear within the first two weeks of postnatal life.

Changes in spatial positions stimulate the sense organs, muscles, and the semicircular canals of the ear. A neonate evidently reacts to spatial changes. When he falls or is held upside down, he makes general postural adjustments. If his body is rotated, his head moves and his eyes oscillate back and forth.

Some degree of sensitivity to pain is present at birth, and it becomes keener during the first few days thereafter. The original response to pain is withdrawal of the area where pain is felt. If a neonate's hand is pricked with a pin, he will draw it away. During the first day, he does this only in response to many pin pricks, but, after a few days, he does so after only a few stimulations. There appear to be constitutional differences in pain sensitivity, or pain tolerance, and female infants generally react more to pain than males. Degree of pain sensitivity may be an important factor in the later acquisition of fears and anxieties.

Perceptual Capacities

Even though a neonate's sense organs function relatively well, it seems unlikely that he *perceives* the world as adults do. Perception involves the organization and interpretation of simple sense impressions, and mature perception requires both further neurological development and learning.

Nevertheless, even very young babies give evidence of some crude, primitive types of perceptual capabilities that are probably inherent. Thus, as we have already learned, neonates follow moving spots of light, indicating that they are able to make at least a primitive differentiation between "figure" and "ground." Moreover, infants two months of age smile at any pattern nodding toward them that approximates the human face, even a grotesque mask. Apparently these moving patterns are discriminated and elicit reactions very early in life, and with few, if any, specific learning experiences. It is possible, therefore, that the ability to discriminate the human face from other objects is innate.

Infants are also capable of perceiving drop-off. In one experiment, babies a few months of age were placed, individually, in the center of a heavy, solid glass rectangle. Extending from the center on one side was a checkerboard pattern, placed directly beneath the glass. On the other side, the same kind of pattern was placed several feet below the glass, thus giving the illusion of depth or a visual cliff. If the child's mother came to the shallow end of the table and called to him, the child would readily crawl to her. If she called him from the deep side, however, he would not cross the cliff or approach her, *even though he could pat the glass and knew that the surface was solid.* This suggests that the perception of depth may be innate. If it is not innate, clearly it is learned very early.

Compared with an adult's rich and complex perceptions, however, a neonate's are probably vague, undifferentiated, and diffuse. Jean Piaget, the brilliant Swiss psychologist, suggests that infants a few months of age do not even distinguish themselves and their actions from objects involved in these actions. His own research data indicate that the important changes in perception with age are the result of an active process of elaboration of sense impressions derived from the environment. Gradually, through the experience of sensing things in different ways (for example, seeing, touching, and sucking them) and realizing that objects can appear, disappear, and reappear, an infant begins to distinguish between himself and external objects and events.

All in all (on the basis of many research studies) it seems probable that we learn to perceive in much the same manner as we learn to walk. In both cases the physical and neurological mechanisms that make the learning possible are inherent in the organism; in both cases the basic drive, the urge to put these mechanisms to work, is equally a part of the basic equipment with which nature has endowed us. Our tools are the combined experiences derived from the simultaneous operation of many sense organs in a world where the physical laws are stable.*

Like other kinds of learning, perceptual learning depends on motivation. A very young baby will smile at any figure resembling a face, but a six-month-old differentiates strangers' and parents' faces, smiling at the latter, which are associated with gratification of his needs. Infants do not ordinarily pay much attention to colors, although they can discriminate among them. But a six-month-old easily learns to reach for a blue bottle that contains a sweet-tasting formula and to reject a red bottle that previously contained bitter liquids. In other words, undifferentiated aspects of an infant's environment may become salient by virtue of being associated with pleasant or unpleasant stimuli. When this occurs, they are attended to, differentiated, and perceived. In this sense, a good deal of perception is *learned.*

Although it is not possible to specify the relative contributions of maturation and learning to perceptual development, it is clear that both are involved. "We do not completely learn to perceive nor is perception completely innate." †

Motor Responses

At birth, an infant can make an astonishing number of motor responses. Psychologists assume that these depend on maturation alone, since they appear independently of learning or practice. Apparently they emerge as a result of biological changes, such as increase in size and complexity of the nervous system, and general anatomical and physiological growth.

Some of these responses have survival value, assisting the neonate in adjusting to the new external environment—keeping him nourished and healthy, and, to some extent, protecting him from noxious or damaging stimuli. For example, at birth, when their lips (or cheeks) are stimulated, almost all babies make sucking movements which enable them to obtain nourishment from a breast or bottle. The *pupillary reflex* (contraction of the pupils in reaction to bright lights or flashes) is present at birth, and provides protection from potential harm. Other survival-value responses that neonates manifest include: head-mouth orientation movements ("searching" movements that help an infant find a nipple), swallowing, opening and closing the eyes, coughing, vomiting unwanted food, and turning away the face from an irritating or painful stimulus.

A neonate is also capable of a number of localized, specific responses. The *grasp* reflex—tight closing of the hand when it is stimulated by contact or

* Goodenough, F. L., and Tyler, L. E. *Developmental psychology.* New York: Appleton-Century-Crofts, 1959, p. 264.

† Solley, C. M., and Murphy, G. *Development of the perceptual world.* New York: Basic Books, 1960, p. 131.

pressure on the palm—is strong at birth but weakens within a few weeks. If the sole of an infant's foot is stroked, he exhibits the *Babinski reflex*—extending the big toe and fanning out the others. A two-week-old infant, placed face downward in a prone position, will lift his head so that his chin is raised. Stroking the inner thigh of male babies will produce penis erection and the raising of the testes.

Many mass, generalized responses are also included in his behavior repertoire. A neonate can shiver, tremble, squirm, twist, and arch his back. Sudden stimulation by loud noises, falling, or application of hot or cold stimuli, elicits a *startle response*—throwing the arms apart and the head back and extending the legs.

Motor Development during the First Year

Motor development proceeds at an extraordinary pace after the neonatal period. It follows a definite sequence, generally proceeding in cephalocaudal and proximodistal directions. Maturation and learning continue to be intimately interrelated in the acquisition of motor skills.

In one longitudinal study, the motor abilities of 60 boys and girls were observed repeatedly at frequent intervals from birth through 36 months of age. This study yielded the California Infant Scale of Motor Development, which consists of 76 items of motor behavior with their age placements—that is, the age in months at which the development is normally found. The scale provides a basis for evaluating a particular child's progress in motor development—whether he is average, accelerated, or retarded.

TABLE 1

The California Infant Scale of Motor Development

Test Items	*Age Placement (months)*	*Test Items*	*Age Placement (months)*
Crawling movements	.2	Rolls from back to stomach	7.0
Lifts head at shoulder	.5	Complete thumb opposition	7.6
Retains red ring	.7	Fine prehension of pellet	9.3
Arm thrusts in play	1.7	Raises self to sitting position	9.4
Leg thrusts in play	1.8	Early stepping movements	9.6
Head erect and steady	2.9	Stands up	10.6
Turns from side to back	3.4	Walks with help	11.6
Sits with support	3.5	Sits down	12.5
Sits with slight support	4.6	Walks alone	13.0
Turns from back to side	5.0	Jumps off floor; both feet	28.0
Effort to sit	5.4	Walks on tiptoe	30.1
Pulls to sitting position	6.2	Walks upstairs, alternating forward foot	35.5
Sits alone 30" or more	6.2		

From Table I, p. 3, of Bayley, N. *The development of motor abilities during the first three years,* Monographs of the Society for Research in Child Development, Monograph No. 1, 1936.

Developments in specific abilities, such as prehension (grasping), manipulation, crawling, creeping, and walking, have also received systematic study. Analysis of detailed moving pictures of babies reaching for, and grasping, a cube demonstrates that manipulative ability evolves through a sequence of stages, proceeding in proximodistal and mass-to-specific directions. An infant's earliest attempts to reach, at approximately 20 weeks of age, are slow and awkward movements, with many unnecessary actions of the shoulders, upper arms, and elbows. With development, superfluous action is eliminated, reaching becomes more direct, and the originally crude movements of the wrist, hand, and fingers become much more precise. Psychologists have also carefully investigated the sequence of development of posture and locomotion. These are illustrated in Figure 1, which gives the ages at which half the children studied attained each stage.

Most aspects of motor development progress in an orderly sequence, but some infants have slight reversals in the phases, or skip some phases entirely. Moreover, among children there are marked individual differences in age of attaining various stages, and the transition from one stage to the next is not always smooth. Immature responses, for instance, may crop up occasionally even after the achievement of more mature ones. Acceleration or retardation in motor development, however, has very little relationship to later intelligence, as measured by intelligence tests.

Maturation plainly plays an extremely prominent role in the acquisition of motor skills. Evidence for this is found in normal development of postural responses and locomotion despite severe restrictions on early practice. For example, a pair of girl twins who, for their first nine months, were confined to their cribs, lying on their backs so that they could not practice sitting or standing, exhibited motor responses such as raising the head and turning to one side at the normal ages. One of the twins suffered no retardation in standing or walking independently.

Among Hopi Indians, infants' motor activities are traditionally severely restricted. They are kept bound to cradleboards (which their mothers carry) most of the time for the first three months and for part of each day after that. Yet, Hopi children reared in this traditional way begin to walk at approximately the same time as children who have not been so restricted. These studies show that the initial appearance of these early motor skills depends primarily on innate maturational factors rather than on learning or practice.

Furthermore, these skills cannot be taught until an infant has become sufficiently mature for them, that is, until his neuromuscular apparatus has "ripened" to a certain point. That this is so was demonstrated in the following experiment. The investigators attempted, by training, to accelerate the development of stair climbing and the building of towers with cubes. The subjects were a pair of identical twins, 46 weeks old, the normal age for the initial appearance of these particular skills. One was given six weeks of daily practice sessions in the two activities, while her twin, the control, had no contact with stairs or with cubes until she was 53 weeks old. The control

Figure 1. The development of posture and locomotion in infants. (From Shirley, M. M. The first two years, a study of twenty-five babies: *Vol. II,* Intellectual Development. Inst. Child Welfare Monogr. Ser. No. *8. Minneapolis: University of Minnesota Press, 1933. With permission of the University of Minnesota Press.)*

was then given two weeks of training. At the end of this time, she equalled or surpassed her twin. The investigators concluded that "there is no conclusive evidence that practice and exercise even hasten the actual appearance of [these] types of reaction. . . . The time of appearance is fundamentally determined by the ripeness of the neural structures." *

Under normal conditions, a child will sit, walk, climb stairs, and build with

* Gesell, A., and Thompson, H. Learning and growth in identical infant twins: an experimental study by the method of co-twin control. *Genet. Psychol. Monogr.,* 1929, 5,1–124, p. 114.

blocks when he attains the necessary degree of maturation, even though the opportunities for earlier learning have been restricted. But the role of practice and learning in the further development of these skills must not be underestimated. Once the infant acquires these basic motor skills, practice and learning bring improvements. For example, in walking, coordination improves, waste movements become eliminated, and steps become longer, straighter, and more rapid. Similarly, the movements involved in manipulation become less awkward, more direct and more precise.

Infant Speech

The essential components of speech, the elementary sounds, are called *phonemes*. These may be defined as the smallest units of speech that make a difference to a listener or a speaker. Actually, no two sounds are identical in every respect and, within each phoneme, there are many variations or "free variants"—that is, sounds that may be substituted for one another without altering their meaning. Thus, the letter *b* in the word *ball* is recognizable whether it is delivered in a high pitched or low pitched voice, whispered, drawn out, shouted, or sung. But there are some features of phonemes that are relatively invariant and distinctive, and these can be described by linguists in terms of both acoustic and articulational similarities—that is, they must be heard and sounded in distinctive ways. Although a number of them emerge spontaneously in a child's earliest vocalizations, further maturation and learning result in increased similarity between the phonemes pronounced by the child and those pronounced by adults in his culture.

Painstaking recording of all the sounds produced by young infants shows that those under two months of age can utter about seven phonemes. By six months, the average infant uses 12 phonemes; and at one year, 18, or about half the number included in adult American speech. During the first year the number of vowel sounds exceeds the number of consonant sounds, but the proportion of vowels to consonants becomes gradually reduced until, during the second year, consonants become more numerous. Adults have a consonant-vowel ratio of 1.4:1.

Early sound production is largely a motor function, and like other motor abilities, its development follows a definite sequence that strongly suggests a maturational basis. For example, sounds formed at the back of the mouth, such as *h*, ordinarily appear first, but decrease in relative frequency as sounds involving the use of the teeth and lips become more common. Furthermore, children of all nations and cultures make the same sounds, and in the same order. English and American infants pronounce French nasals and the French guttural *r* as well as German vowel sounds. These later disappear—much to the despair of high school language teachers—presumably because they are not heard as part of the child's everyday environment and hence are not encouraged, rewarded, or practiced.

Maturation sets the pace. With a normal environment the child's speech awaits a step-by-step unfolding of the growth process. Consequently we find a succession of developmental stages that are quite similar in all children. By manipulating the language environment of the child we can modify or delay the development but we shall never teach a baby to utter prepositional phrases before he begins to babble. The successive stages of language development are similar in all normal children.*

On the average, babies pronounce recognizable syllables by the third month. As a child matures, his syllables become sharper, clearer, and more distinct. Cooing and babbling, repeating the same sound over and over again, like "da da da" and "ga ga ga," begin at about this time and continue until about the end of the first year. Early babblings are probably not attempted imitations of adults' speech, but rather sounds the child makes for his own amusement. Toward the end of the first half year, the infant is likely to "talk" to his parents and other familiar people when he is being played with or talked to. Imitation of sounds made by others generally begins after approximately nine months.

The motivations impelling a baby's imitation of others' speech are not yet fully understood. Imitation may be learned because imitative responses are rewarded directly by such events as the mother smiling, cooing, or picking him up. One learning theorist, O. H. Mowrer, has suggested that the baby's imitative responses acquire *secondary reward value.* This means that pronouncing sounds that are similar to his mother's is rewarding because these sounds are associated with the rewards and tension reduction provided by her. When the baby hears himself making sounds like his mother's, he, in effect, re-experiences some of the rewarding, nurturant, warm relationships he has with his mother.

A baby does not generally learn new sounds by imitation, but imitates only those sounds that have already occurred spontaneously in his babbling. Through imitation, however, the child begins to select certain sound combinations and to apply these sound combinations to particular situations in which he has heard others use them. During the last months of the first year, the child forms meaningful associations between words and what they stand for. This marks the beginning of true language, that is, of language as a means of social communication.

At about 10 months, a baby can respond to simple commands. The average baby speaks his first word, a single or duplicated syllable ("mama" or "dada"), sometime around the end of the first year. At this time, a single word may function as a whole sentence. For example, "dada" may mean "where is daddy," "I want daddy," or "give me that, daddy." This is the period of the single-word sentence.

Marked individual differences in speech development are apparent right from the start—differences in frequency and variety of speech sounds emitted,

* Miller, G. A. *Language and communication.* New York: McGraw-Hill, 1951, p. 141.

duration of the babbling phase, elaboration of sounds and inflections, and vocabulary development. These differences are due in part to variations in rates of maturation, but, even in the first few months, environmental factors also exert a significant impact. For example, infants under six months living in an unstimulating orphanage environment, compared with those living in families, tend to be retarded in frequency, number, and types of sounds emitted. There is experimental evidence, too, that rewarding an infant for making sounds, by smiling at him and stroking his abdomen, produces an increase in the amount of vocalization.

Babies between six months and a year of age from middle-class families make more varied and more frequent sounds than infants from laboring-class families. This is presumably because middle-class mothers are more likely to reward and encourage their children's vocalizations. These lines of evidence all strongly suggest that an infant's speech development can be stimulated or retarded through environment and experience.

PHYSICAL GROWTH IN CHILDHOOD

After the period of extremely rapid development in the first two years, over-all growth proceeds more gradually. Growth of the upper parts of the body slows down, while the legs continue to grow particularly rapidly during the preschool years. By the age of six, a child's general body proportions closely resemble an adult's. Incidentally, there is a significant correlation between an individual's height as a young child and his adult height. In general, tall children will be tall adults.

Changes in build between the age of six and adolescence are relatively slight and are largely the result of the lengthening of the limbs. After the age of six, growth proceeds at a relatively slow pace for sometime. Up to the tenth year, boys are, on the average, taller than girls, but between the ages of 10 and 15, girls are somewhat taller and heavier than boys. Girls are apt to gain height at a rapid rate from 9 to 12 years, while boys do so from 11 to 14. Just before adolescence, at an average age of 12 for girls and 14 for boys, there is normally a "growth spurt"—a period of extremely rapid gains in height and weight. After adolescence the growth rate slows down considerably, until final height is attained, on the average, for girls by the age of 17, and for boys by 19.

It must be emphasized that there are marked individual variations from these averages in all aspects of growth. Not all children develop in the same way or at the same rates. Some grow relatively more in height while others increase in weight; these variations produce different body types such as tall and slender or short and stocky.

Individual organs and organ systems of the body grow at different rates. During the first three or four years, muscles grow continuously, roughly in proportion to over-all body growth. After this period, muscle size expands rapidly, accounting for about 75 per cent of a child's gain in weight during the fifth and sixth years. During middle childhood, muscle tissue increases in proportion to general growth, and the child gradually gains in strength.

As in most aspects of development, boys tend to be slower than girls in muscular growth. Muscle tissue, for instance, increases most rapidly during adolescence, between the ages of 12 and 15 in girls, between 15 and 16 in boys. The ultimate development of girls' muscles, however, is not as great as boys', so that girls are the physically weaker sex at maturity. After 16, there is little increase in the size or weight of the muscles. In adulthood, the total weight of muscle tissue is about 40 times what it was at birth.

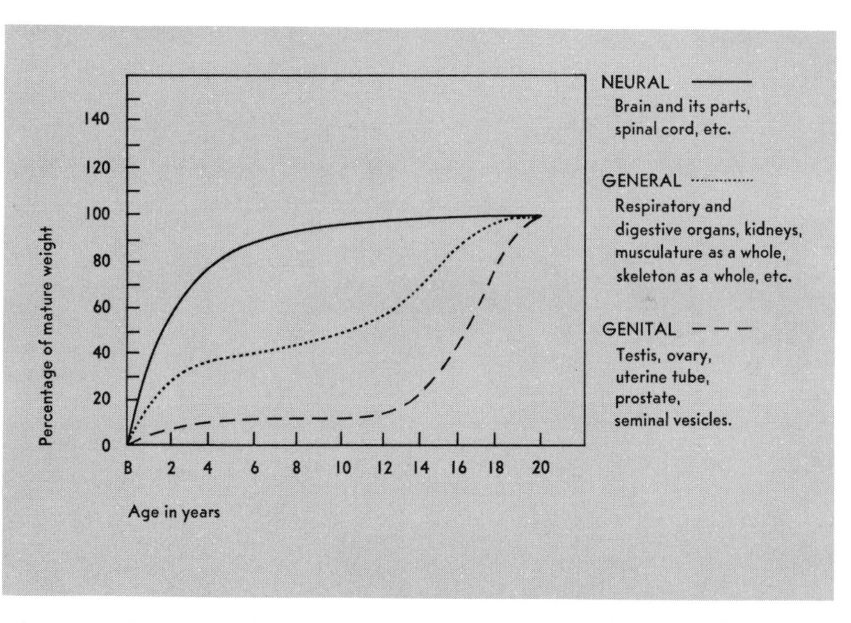

Figure 2. Curves showing growth rates of the three major categories of organs, or tissue types, in the human body. (Adapted from Scammon, R. E., in Morris' human anatomy. *New York: P. Blakiston's Sons & Co. Copyright, 1923.)*

Figure 2 shows the curves of postnatal growth rates of three major types of organs. *General body tissue* (including bones, muscles, and most of the internal organs) grows rapidly at first, and then at a decelerated rate until about two years before adolescence; then the preadolescent spurt brings a second period of speedy growth; finally, a slowdown occurs until adult size is attained. Development of the *nervous* (*or neural*) *system* is extremely rapid during the first six years and then slows down sharply—on a graph this is called a negatively accelerated growth curve. In marked contrast to the neural system, the *genital system* has a positively accelerated curve: a period of very slow growth during childhood, and extremely rapid development at puberty.

PHYSICAL CHANGES OF ADOLESCENCE

The dramatic changes of adolescence are precipitated by a number of changes in the glands, which result in increased production of male hormones in boys and female hormones in girls. The sudden, rapid increase in the size of the genital organs, and the attainment of sexual maturity, mark the onset of puberty, the first phase of adolescence. This phase is generally dated from the first menstruation (menarche) in girls, and the emergence of pigmented pubic hair in boys.

On the average, puberty is attained between 13 and 14 years of age but there are wide individual variations. A small percentage of boys reach puberty at 10 and are fully sexually mature by 14, while some have not yet begun to show any signs of adolescence by the latter age and do not attain complete maturity until they are 19 or 20. Analogously, a few girls reach menarche as early as the age of 10 but, in a few exceptional cases, the event may be delayed until 19 or 20.

Between the onset of the growth spurt and menarche, a girl's vagina and uterus develop rapidly; however, the ovaries, which are the primary sex glands, increase in size *after* menarche, particularly between the seventeenth and twentieth years. Breasts begin to bud during puberty, and grow rapidly until they reach full maturity at 18 or 19.

The primary male sex characteristics, the testes and the penis, grow at a highly accelerated rate during adolescence, usually attaining their mature size at about 17 or 18. At the same time, a boy's pubic hair becomes coarser and denser and shows pigmentation. Growth of hair in the arm pits, on the face, and finally on the trunk, arms, and legs, follows. Voice changes in a boy start about the time he reaches puberty, but may not be completed until a few years later.

Facial proportions also change in adolescence. The forehead tends to become higher and wider, the mouth to widen, and the lips to become fuller. A boy's face is likely to become angular and harder, while a girl's assumes a softer and more rounded contour. In general, the changes occur later among boys than among girls.

Various aspects of physical maturation during adolescence tend to be interrelated, although there are individual exceptions. For example, an individual who has a relatively early growth spurt will generally reach puberty early.

Developments of the primary and secondary sexual characteristics are also closely related.

The attainment of sexual maturity, and the accompanying increase in sex drive during adolescence, may precipitate some major adjustment problems. How the adolescent learns to handle his recently strengthened sex drives will depend on his personal history, social-class background, and general social adjustment. In the middle class, sexual intercourse before marriage is frowned upon, so that an adolescent from this group is likely to have strong conflicts about the expression of his sexual interests. In contrast, the lower-class adolescent will probably experience less conflict about this problem, since there are fewer restrictions on adolescent sexual relationships in that class. According to extensive data on sexual behavior, before marriage, the overwhelming majority of males engage in at least exploratory sexual activities, to the point of orgasm, but premarital sexual relations are less common among girls.

It would, of course, be a gross oversimplification to attribute all an adolescent's problems and conflicts to his increased sex drives. In our culture, a great number of demands press upon the adolescent simultaneously; many "developmental tasks" must be handled in a short period of time. Consider the following: Adolescents are expected to achieve some emotional independence from their families; to select and prepare for occupations; to ready themselves for marriage and family life; and to assume social responsibilities and adopt an acceptable code of moral and ethical ideals and behavior. In view of the vast number of difficult problems he must face—usually with inadequate preparation—it is hardly surprising that many an adolescent experiences intense conflicts. His methods of coping with them will depend on many factors, including his relationships with his parents and peers, his school adjustment, his intellectual level, the expectancies of others (parents, peers, and social-class group), and even, to some extent, the rate at which he matures physically.

PHYSICAL GROWTH AND BEHAVIOR

An individual's behavior is, at least to some extent, influenced by his physical characteristics and body structure. Few psychologists subscribe to the theory that body build and personality are closely related; yet there is little doubt that, indirectly, physique affects the development of personality characteristics, attitudes, and emotions. For example, a child who is advanced in physical development for his age is likely to be regarded, and treated, as an older child. His social experiences will therefore be different from those of children whose physical development is slow, and he may be expected to acquire different personality characteristics. A big, well-built, muscular, and well-coordinated boy is more likely than a small one to be a good athlete. For this reason, he may enjoy great social prestige and popularity, and these may foster self-confidence, assurance, and generally good adjustment. The smaller boy, who is unsuccessful in athletics, may develop feelings of inadequacy and inferiority, and may withdraw from companionship with others and become isolated. Or he may compensate for his feelings of inferiority by bragging, arguing, and behaving aggressively.

Changes brought about by physical growth may be related to a host of psychological functions. The attainment of sexual maturity at adolescence is accompanied by many changes in interests, attitudes, and motives. In our culture, adolescence is often a period of storm and stress, which may be partially attributable to the anatomical and physiological—particularly glandular—changes in the body. Probably to an even greater degree, the problems of this period stem from the tremendous cultural pressures on adolescents and the reactions of parents and others who expect new and more mature patterns of behavior from physically maturing children.

DETERMINANTS OF PHYSICAL CHARACTERISTICS

On the basis of the striking resemblances between parents and their children, there can be little doubt that many aspects of appearance are inherited. Genetic factors determine such characteristics as sex, eye color, texture and color of skin and hair, and size and shape of the face. Heredity is largely responsible too for an individual's relative height and weight, and for the dimensions of his hand.

But environment may exert strong influences even on these primarily genetically determined characteristics. For example, the American-born children of Jewish and Japanese immigrants grow taller and weigh more than their parents or their brothers and sisters born abroad. Children of the present generation in the United States and other Western countries are taller and heavier, and grow more rapidly, than children of earlier generations. Maximum height is now attained as much as two years earlier than it was two or three generations ago. All these data suggest that physique and rate of growth are influenced by environmental factors, especially those related to nutrition and living conditions.

Although weight is influenced by heredity, extreme obesity or thinness may be the outcome of glandular disorders, diet, or emotional problems. Overeating may have its roots in emotional maladjustment stemming from parental overprotection or unsatisfactory social relationships. Under these circumstances, food may assume undue importance, and security may be sought in eating or overeating. Analogously, chronic anxiety, worry, fatigue, or glandular disorders may keep an individual's body lean or even emaciated.

Physiological traits and the rate of physical maturation are also in large measure a function of hereditary factors. Identical girl twins tend to reach their first menstruation at the same age. Again, however, environmental forces such as serious illness, dietary deficiencies, or emotional upset may have a significant impact, delaying the age of puberty or retarding the rate of maturation.

Cognitive Development

Cognition refers to the "higher mental processes," that is, to the functions involved in understanding and dealing with the world about us—perception, language, concept formation, abstraction, problem solving, intelligence, and thinking. Originally, psychologists tried to differentiate cognition from emotion, motivation, and personality characteristics, but the distinction is difficult to maintain, for these latter factors may have strong impacts on cognitive functioning. For example, data from a number of systematic studies show that anxiety tends to impair children's problem-solving ability. Those who are highly anxious, lacking in self-

4

confidence, and fearful of failure have much more difficulty in problem-solving tests involving both concrete and abstract problems than children of the same intelligence level who have relatively little anxiety. The differences between highly anxious and nonanxious children are particularly marked when the tasks are difficult or require creative solutions or when the test situation is a threatening one.

In this chapter we shall discuss the major age trends in the development of various aspects of cognition, or the "higher mental processes," and the final section of the chapter will present a brief summary of Piaget's thoughtful and challenging views of general intellectual development. Although each aspect of cognition will receive separate treatment, the cognitive processes actually develop concurrently; moreover, they are interdependent and interactive. For example, progress in language permits, and paves the way for, further advances in concept formation and problem solution. Certain processes, indeed, are so closely interrelated that they can hardly be distinguished from one another. Perception and concept formation, for example, both involve the organization and interpretation of sensory impressions and experiences. Still we can separate them for study on the basis of the complexity of organization involved. Let's start with perception.

THE DEVELOPMENT OF PERCEPTION

Contrasts Between Infantile and Adult Perception

A neonate's perceptions are, compared with an adult's, diffuse and disorganized. Yet, even within the first half year, an infant is capable of perceiving depth and of differentiating figure from ground, simple from complex patterns, and friendly from unfriendly faces. With greater neurological maturity and increased perceptual learning, the child's early undifferentiated, or global, perceptions become more precise and differentiated, sharper, and more like adults'. The ability to perceive details and relationships among parts is generally acquired over an extended period of time. For only through experience do the various components and aspects of the world become related to one another in new ways and in new integrations.

> The adult has a kind of many-dimensioned map or ground plan of the world he moves in, a sense that it exists even if he is not there. For the adult (but not at all for the infant) objects exist in an organized world in which he distinguishes (fairly well) reality and fantasy, as well as up and down and sideways, or past, present and future. In addition, some objects exist in the social network with countless subtle relationships of blood, respect, duty, affection, envy, role, status, power, etc.*

* Stone, L. J., and Church, J. *Childhood and adolescence.* New York: Random House, 1957, p. 85. © Copyright 1957 by Random House, Inc. Reprinted by permission.

The adult's "ground map" is developed largely through years of learning and experience. As Piaget has pointed out, understanding the world involves *active* exploration of the environment and continual organization and reorganization of sense impressions derived from it.

We have only limited and spotty knowledge of the complex perceptual changes occurring between infancy and adulthood, and of the processes underlying them. The following sections provide some samples of research findings on trends in the development of perception, but there are many crucial problems in this area that are still unsolved. We know practically nothing, for instance, of the *processes* involved in the organization and integration of early sense impressions. Are there specific types of experiences that can accelerate or retard perceptual development? What neural mechanisms account for improvements in perception? Does the ability to make one type of perceptual discrimination facilitate the learning of others, and if so, how much? How far and how fast can youngsters' abilities to form concepts be "pushed"? There are as yet no adequate answers to these and many other questions.

Form Perception

Young infants can perceive, and react to, differences in the shapes of objects. In one ingenious experiment, babies between six and 15 months of age were presented with blocks of different forms (circles, crosses, and triangles) that they could handle and lick. One of them, the "correct" one, was sweetened with saccharine. Infants as young as six months old were able to discriminate among the forms, and soon learned to choose the desirable, sweet one. Changes in the relative positions or spatial orientations of the various forms did not affect discrimination significantly.

Interest in form develops early. If you give an 18-month-old child a formboard test (a test in which loose blocks of varied shapes are to be fitted into depressions in a base), he will try to place the figures into the available holes, but he will pay little attention to whether the form fits the hole. A three-year-old, however, is likely to use a simple formboard properly on the first trial.

In one study, given equal opportunity to match objects by color and form, children between two and three showed a marked preference for matching forms. From three to six, color became more potent, but after six, and continuing through adulthood, form again became more important.

Ability to discriminate among forms as complex as numbers and as the letters of the alphabet develops gradually and is fairly well established by the age of five. Recent experimental evidence indicates that visual discrimination of graphemes, or letter-like forms (for example, ◁, ⊥, ᑫ), improves continuously from ages four to eight. As would be anticipated, there are wide individual differences at all ages studied. Many six- and seven-year-olds may have difficulty in making such fine distinctions as those between p and q, b and d, 3 and E.

Just as phonemes (see page 24) have invariant features which must be heard and responded to, letters and numbers have distinctive, critical features to which a child must become sensitive. Improvements in making these visual discriminations, resulting from greater maturity and increased practice in the detection of invariants, play a critical role in the child's learning to read.

Perception of Parts, Wholes, and Details

Young children do not ordinarily differentiate the parts of what they perceive, especially if the stimuli are unfamiliar or have no meaning for them. They perceive largely in terms of context. In general, the ability to extract or differentiate parts from an originally undifferentiated global perception develops gradually with increasing age.

A baby's mother and father are certainly familiar to him, yet he may not recognize them if they are dressed in costume or in formal clothing. Apparently, the infant has not *differentiated* the critical or distinctive characteristics of the parents (facial features, physique, and so on) from the total context generally associated with them. Gradually, though, he will develop percepts of his father and mother that are independent of this context.

The increase of differentiation of stimuli with age is illustrated (see Figure 3) in this example by Mussen, Conger, and Kagan.

Figure 3. Design used in testing perception of whole and parts. (From Mussen, P. H., Conger, J. J., and Kagan, J. S. Child development and personality. *New York: Harper & Row, 1963, p. 249.)*

> . . . If a four-year-old child is shown [the following design] and asked to describe what he sees, he is apt to say, "A box with lines" or "a design." A seven-year-old is more likely to mention the black circle, "There's a black circle and some lines" or "There's a design with a black hole at the bottom." If the stimulus is an ambiguous ink blot, the five-year-old is likely to attend to [perceive] the whole, and to ignore the parts of the stimulus.*

* Mussen, P. H., Conger, J. J., and Kagan, J. S. *Child development and personality.* New York: Harper & Row, 1963, p. 249.

Thus, he is likely to respond to an inkblot stimulus with some vague, diffuse term such as "dirt," "clay," or "water." An eight-year-old is much more likely to respond to some component part of the stimulus, mentioning specific objects, animals, people, or parts of the body, and describing some details.

The gradual development of the ability to extract details or parts from a whole has also been demonstrated experimentally in studies involving embedded figures. In these studies small objects or figures, known to the subjects, are camouflaged by being embedded in a larger, more complex pattern (see Figure 4 for illustration).

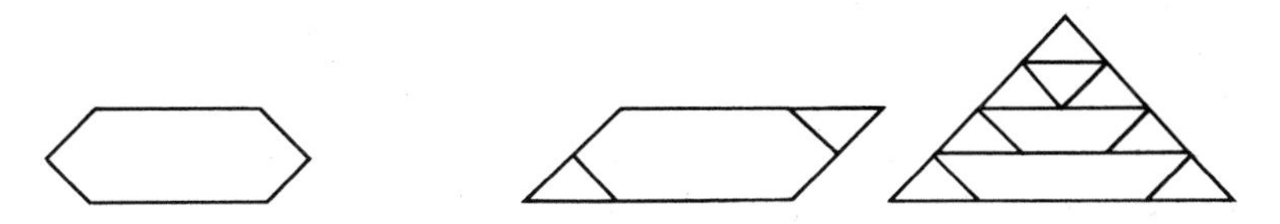

Figure 4. An example of an embedded figure. The shape to the left appears in both the other forms.

Compared with adults, children find it difficult to find embedded figures. In one study, children between five-and-a-half and six-and-a-half years of age were presented with two familiar geometrical figures embedded in more complex figures, and asked to find the familiar figures in the new configuration. Only highly intelligent children were able to do this, and then only with relatively simple new configurations. Less intelligent children were unable to detect the figures at all.

Children between eight and ten years of age may also have difficulty extracting known figures from unfamiliar contexts. Performance in this task improves markedly between the ages of 10 and 13, though, and continues to develop until the age of 17, according to a number of relevant studies. Clearly, then, the ability to differentiate the part from the whole continues to improve throughout adolescence.

The Perceptual Constancies

For adults, the characteristics of objects appear to be remarkably constant in spite of variations in the conditions under which they are perceived. A book ten feet away looks approximately the same as it does when it is five feet away, although, in the first situation, it projects a retinal image (picture on the innermost, neural membrane of the eyeball) that is only half the size of the second (size constancy). Moreover, a book is perceived as a book, regardless of the angle from which it is viewed—from seated, standing, or upsidedown positions (form constancy). The "true" brightness of an object is generally judged fairly accurately regardless of the brightness of its surroundings (brightness constancy). Thus, a piece of coal in strong sunlight may reflect more light than a piece of quartz in deep shade; yet we perceive the coal as darker than the quartz if we perceive their settings. As a result of maturation and learning, the adult is able to attend principally to the invariant and distinctive features—the critical attributes—of the object. He is able to discount the varying, irrelevant aspects of the stimulus situation—differences in distance, directions of viewing, and reflected light.

These constancies develop gradually, however, and improve with age. In one study, infants between 10 and 50 weeks of age were presented simultaneously with two rattles, one close and another, three times as large, three times as far away. The two rattles cast images of equal size on the retina, but they did not elicit identical responses. Infants six months of age and older reached for the nearer rattle far more frequently than for the other one. Apparently, however, size constancy was not well established before the age of six months.

In one excellent experiment on size constancy, subjects were instructed to manipulate a distant disc that was mechanically adjustable until it appeared to be the same size as a standard disc placed about a yard away. Perfect constancy is achieved when the comparison disc is adjusted to exactly the same size as the standard. Even at the age of two, the earliest age tested, a considerable degree of size constancy is evident, but there is gradual improvement with age until nearly perfect constancy is achieved at about ten.

Brightness and form constancy have also been studied by methods analogous to that in the size-constancy experiment. Brightness constancy turns out to be poor among two-year-olds, but it improves fairly rapidly, although it is far from perfect even at ten. The developmental trend for form constancy is very much like the one for brightness constancy.

CONCEPT FORMATION

The line between percepts and concepts is a fine one, and it is difficult to make a clear-cut distinction between them. Generally, psychologists regard perceptions as organizations of simple sense impressions (visual, auditory, tactile) whereas concept formation involves discovering and defining the critical features common to a group of objects or events. Concepts have been defined as

> . . . organizing systems which serve to bring pertinent features of past experience to bear upon a present stimulus-object. Assuming that stimulus has some effect upon the person (he perceives it) there are evoked processes whereby the object is interpreted, given meaning, and linked with the other concurrent activities of the organism. These processes do not occur at random, but in a more or less systematic

and consistent manner. In short, prior experience with objects equips a person to react similarly to objects of the same name and related kinds. In defining the properties of concepts we are really identifying the ways in which experience is organized. . . . Although concepts are usually given a verbal label (the name, for instance, of a stimulus-object) the concept itself is actually a complex system of internal activities which represent the impressions, feelings, and responses associated with that object.*

Obviously a child's store of concepts depends on his culture and past experiences, for these define the variety and types of concepts available to him. If wigwams or igloos are unknown or have no labels in his culture, the child can form no concepts of these things. An American child acquires only one concept for rice; an Indonesian child has labels for, and differentiates, many types of rice: rice in the paddies, mature rice, boiled rice, fried rice, and so forth.

Skill in concept formation is closely linked to the acquisition of language, particularly to labeling. After he has learned the names or labels applied to objects or events, a child is likely to react in the same way to all stimuli having the same labels. This is known as *verbal mediation* or *mediated generalization*. Numerous experiments demonstrate that such mediation is of paramount importance in concept formation, problem solving, thinking, and learning.

To illustrate, in transposition experiments subjects learn to make choices on the basis of *relationships* among stimuli. Suppose, for example, a child first learns to choose the *largest* of three squares. Later, he is presented with three different squares, the smallest of them being the same size as the largest, or correct, one of the previous trials. Young children, with limited language ability, find it very difficult to learn to respond to the relative sizes of the objects. Instead, they choose in terms of the absolute size of the stimulus. Older children who know—and can apply—words (verbal mediators) like "largest" or "middle-size," learn transposition or relational choices very easily.

Abstraction and concept formation are required for successful *reversal learning* in which a child must learn to do the opposite of what he has previously done in the same situation. To illustrate, experimental subjects may be taught to discriminate between two stimuli that differ in both size and color. Choice of the larger of two blocks, regardless of its color, is rewarded; that is, the size dimension is relevant and color is irrelevant. Subsequently there is a reversal shift in pattern of rewards in the experiment; the size dimension is still the relevant one but the child is rewarded for choosing the smaller rather than the larger block. (In nonreversal shifts the previously irrelevant dimension becomes pertinent. Whereas rewards had previously depended on discriminating along the size dimension, they would now be contingent on choices based on color.)

* Vinacke, W. E. Concept formation in children of school ages. *Educ.*, 1954, 74, 527–534, p. 529.

Children who can make mediating verbal responses—who can say to themselves, "It's the size that's important"—find it relatively easy to learn the reversal shift. Experimental data show that as verbal skills improve, reversal shifts are mastered more easily. They are relatively difficult for nursery school children, and few of them readily learn to shift. Among kindergarten children, those who are fast learners (presumably bright, verbal children) have little difficulty mastering reversal shifts; slow learners do not learn the shift as easily.

If preschool children are taught to verbalize the relevant dimension (to say "large" when making the discrimination), they can master the reversal shift, but children who learn to verbalize the irrelevant dimension or do not make any mediating response find the task difficult. Among children between three and ten years of age who were subjects in a complex experimental study, only 25 per cent of the three-year-olds responded on the basis of reversal shift, but this proportion rose gradually with age, 62 per cent of the ten-year-olds responding this way. Apparently the ability to learn reversal shifts depends on having the concept (verbal mediation) of the critical dimension, and, this, in turn, improves with greater skill in language.

Age Trends in Concept Formation

Two types of organization of concepts are distinguishable: horizontal and vertical. The former includes concepts approximately equal in inclusiveness (such as, dog, cat, and horse), the latter includes concepts of progressively more inclusiveness (Spotty, dog, animal). A child's earliest concepts are generally of the horizontal type, and like his early perceptions, they are broad and undifferentiated, reflecting his limited experience and language facility. Vague concepts such as *doggie* are applied not only to dogs, but to a variety of objects that have some degree of resemblance to dogs, such as cats, rabbits, and pictures of animals.

With more precise perceptions, more varied experiences, and increased vocabulary, a child's concepts become more refined, and more sharply differentiated. By the time the child is two or three years old, dog and horse, boy and girl, have become mutually exclusive concepts, but they are still *concrete,* attached to real objects and their external characteristics. A child of this age cannot yet describe or compare concepts.

Concrete concepts become *true concepts* when the child can do something with them beyond attaching them to concrete realities, when he can compare them, combine them, describe them—that is, *think and talk about their attributes.* (True concepts are likely to appear first in the later preschool years.) At earlier stages, what was perceived determined what could be named; once conceptual thinking begins, however, the word may determine which things are perceived, which attributes are differentiated and combined. "Doggie" becomes a true concept when the child can deal verbally simultaneously with, say, "doggies" and "kittens": "Doggie bark. Kittie meow." A simple utterance of this sort tells us that the child has abstracted characteristics—the dog's *bark*—generalized them—*all dogs bark*—and compared these characteristics with those of other species—*cats do not bark, they meow.**

Higher-order (vertical) conceptualization is not generally achieved until sometime during the school years. Grouping concepts into abstract categories to form higher-order categories, depends on the recognition of the common elements in these concepts. Yet, according to the data collected in the standardization of intelligence tests, the ability to see similarities is not well developed until school age. In the Stanford-Binet intelligence test, the item "In what way are apple and peach alike?" is a seven-year-old item—that is, it can be answered by the average seven-year-old.

By the time he enters the first grade, a child has a large variety of concepts pertaining to his physical environment, animate and inanimate objects, toys, games, his home, and family. As for numbers and abstract ideas, however, he is just beginning to form concepts. The first few years of school are of critical importance in the child's conceptual development, yet it is impossible to evaluate precisely the influence of the school in this development.

Up to the age of six, the child's concepts are determined mainly by his own specific experiences and actions, and are, consequently, naive, inconsistent, diffuse, imprecise, simple, and closely bound up with the immediate perceptual features of objects. Perhaps as a result of marked improved verbal skills, a marked shift occurs at about the age of six. Concepts become more logical and differentiated, a trend that continues throughout the school years and into adult life. "It seems likely that, given the necessary knowledge, practice, and vocabulary, the child of six can form many concepts essentially similar to those of adults, qualified by his lack of experience and skill in applying them." †

A sample of developmental trends in some important types of concepts follows.

Quantitative Concepts. Two- and three-year-olds have strikingly naive quantitative concepts. They understand more than and less than, bigger and smaller, some and one, but any number more than one is likely to be expressed as two, regardless of actual quantity. During the preschool period, children learn to discriminate between a larger and smaller number of objects, such as groups of dolls or toy cars, and they learn to label collections of two, three, or four articles. And by the time a child is five, he may be able to count objects in small series. Although these achievements are the basic ingredients from which number concepts are derived, they are not quantitative concepts.

The preschool child has only *concrete* concepts determined by his immediate perceptions; he does not understand that total quantity does not change just because parts are rearranged. In one of Piaget's ingenious experi-

* Stone, L. J., and Church, J. *Childhood and adolescence,* pp. 177–178.
† Vinacke, W. E. Concept formation in children of school ages, p. 531.

ments, a child is given equal numbers of vases and flowers and asked to place a flower in each vase. After he has done this, the flowers are removed and grouped together while the vases are spread out over a wide area. When asked whether there are more flowers or vases, children under four tend to say that there are more vases than flowers because they cover a wider area. If the flowers are spread out and the vases bunched, they say there are more flowers. In short, a child of this age does not have any clear concept of the distinctive, or critical, features of quantity. In Piaget's terms, they have not yet acquired the concept of *conservation*.

Intensive systematic research on young children's potential for learning mathematical concepts began only a few years ago, and, at the present time, there are a number of excellent projects in which first- and second-grade pupils are taught basic concepts of geometry, higher mathematics (for example, set theory and lattices), and physics (the concept of force, for instance). Preliminary reports indicate that youngsters are able to master some concepts of higher mathematics much more readily than educators had previously thought. We need more data, however, before we can assess the results of the projects adequately.

Time Concepts. Although time concepts are of great importance to adults, they mean little to young children. Events that occurred only last week are regarded as being in the historical past; the future has no real meaning. Initially, an infant's sense of time is highly concrete, being related to his own routines—eating, sleeping, getting up.

Concepts of time relationships evolve slowly. For example, at four years of age, children begin to know what day of the week it is, at five, the month and the year. Three-year-olds tend to know their own age, four-year-olds the date of their next birthday, five-year-olds how old they are and how old they will be after their next birthday. Judged by adult standards, the preschool child's concepts of time are generally diffuse and uncoordinated.

Concepts of Social Relationships. Since his experience in social relationships is limited, a child's social concepts are rudimentary. A three-year-old generally has few salient social interactions outside his family circle. Hence it is not surprising to find that

> . . . For the preschool child, . . . family relationships are the prototype of all relationships, and these overshadow the less personally significant abstract relationships that adults often deal in. Thus when the child is given a formal classification test consisting of blocks that offer a number of abstract principles for grouping—color, shape, size—he may ignore all of these and instead base his arrangements on the intimate, concrete scheme of his own existence and group the blocks into families, large ones being the "father" and "mother" and smaller ones the "babies." Here the child relies on the attribute of size, but in a concrete way tied to his emotionally relevant reality. Even the concept "family," however, is still indistinctly articulated for the preschool child. A four-year-old, for instance, meeting his teacher's husband, asks "Mr. Jones, are you Mrs. Jones' daddy?" and the next moment,

to Mrs. Jones, "Are you his mommy?" A mere adult cannot really know, of course, whether the child means these relationships to be taken literally, or whether, lacking the concepts "husband" and "wife," he is trying to ask something like "Are you the daddy in the family in which Mrs. Jones is the mommy?" At the same time, children can certainly live quite comfortably with unnoted inconsistencies and contradictions that adults would find very troubling. The lack of abstractness in preschool children's ideas of family may also be observed in the indignant retort of a five-year-old to the assertion that people in the same family cannot marry: 'They can, too! My mommy married my daddy!" *

As a child moves out into the neighborhood, playground, and school, his social experiences broaden tremendously and become more complex and subtle. His perception and comprehension of social relationships expand rapidly, so that by eight or nine, he has acquired a wide range of social concepts pertaining to many kinds of personal relationships.

LANGUAGE DEVELOPMENT

It would be difficult to overestimate the importance of language in a child's development. A major part of his learning—at home, in the neighborhood, in school, and from the mass media—depends on language, which is indeed, the basis of all social communication. The functioning of the social structure and the transmission of culture from one generation to the next depend largely on language.

As we have already noted (see p. 37), the acquisition of words is essential for abstraction and concept formation and, in fact, for almost all higher learning and higher mental processes, such as thinking, planning, reasoning, paying attention, remembering, and judging. Learning to understand and use language, therefore, presents a multiplicity of new opportunities for psychological growth. Failure to become skillful in communication (speaking, understanding, reading, and writing) immeasurably handicaps a child's general intellectual and cognitive development.

Our focus in the present section is on the developmental trends and changes in language ability with increasing age and on some factors related to these changes. The process of language acquisition is not yet fully understood, however. It is obviously strongly influenced by environmental conditions and learning. Yet many linguists feel that learning theory cannot fully explain the complex, amazing, and often extremely rapid development of the child's vocabulary and mastery of grammatical structure and semantics.

As we learned in Chapter 3, the ability to vocalize elementary speech sounds emerges primarily as the result of neuromuscular maturation. But the child must *learn* to use language for communicating with others, for understanding the speech of others, and for thinking.

Recall that a child begins to understand language—to make meaningful

* Stone, L. J., and Church, J. *Childhood and adolescence,* p. 180.

associations between words and what they stand for—late in the first year and that he utters his first word sometime around his first birthday, on the average. In the two- or three-month period immediately following the acquisition of the first few words, however, progress in language is slow. The infant appears to be concentrating on the mastery of motor skills such as walking, and on exploration, to the relative neglect of language.

After this, however, come swift and dramatic improvements. In an "interview" session with an examiner, the average two-year-old in one study spoke 37 different words. This is undoubtedly a minimal estimate of vocabulary size, for the children probably knew more words than they spoke spontaneously in what was, for them, a highly artificial situation. The range of individual differences among the two-year-olds was tremendous: 6 to 126 words.

An infant's *effective* vocabulary, that is, his ability to speak *or* understand words, expands enormously starting with the second year. Table 2 shows the

TABLE 2

Growth of Vocabulary
Between Eight Months and Six Years of Age

Age in Years and Months	*Average Number of Words*
0–8	0
0–10	1
1–0	3
1–3	19
1–6	22
1–9	118
2–0	272
2–6	446
3–0	896
3–6	1222
4–0	1540
4–6	1870
5–0	2072
5–6	2289
6–0	2562

From Smith, M. E. An investigation of the development of the sentence and the extent of vocabulary in young children. *Univ. Iowa Stud. Child Welfare,* 1926, Vol. 3, No. 5.

increase in the size of average effective vocabulary between the ages of eight months and six years. Concomitant with these advances in the use and comprehension of words during the second year, a child's speech becomes more accurate, adultlike, and hence more comprehensible; and his understanding of directions and questions increases.

The structural pattern of speech changes rapidly and markedly during the preschool years. Nouns and interjections together constitute 60 per cent of a child's utterances at 18 months, but smaller proportions as he grows older. Meanwhile, pronouns, verbs, adjectives, conjunctions, and prepositions increase in frequency. Between the ages of two and three, speech consists primarily of nouns, verbs, and adjectives, but includes few pronouns and virtually no connectives. Yet, by the time a child is three-and-a-half or four years old, the distribution of parts of speech in his conversation approximates that in an adult's.

Concomitantly, a child's vocabulary expands greatly, and he uses words more efficiently and more flexibly. Talk becomes more profuse and speech becomes more comprehensible, articulation and pronunciation improving most rapidly between the ages of three and three-and-a-half. By the age of eight, a youngster's pronunciation does not differ significantly from an adult's.

Sentences become progressively longer, more complex, and more elaborate. Two-year-olds are typically in the early sentence stage (average sentence length, 1.2 words), stating simple requests and descriptions of the environment, generally lacking in auxiliaries, articles, connectives, and prepositions. In the short-sentence stage, at about three-and-a-half, sentences averaging three-and-a-half to four-and-a-half words are used, but only a half year later, at about four years of age on the average, children use complete sentences, six to eight words in length. These sentences tend to be more definite and more complex, containing more relational words, than those of earlier periods. A child may not be able to express the rules of usage, but it is obvious from his speech that he knows how to form plurals, past and future tenses, subordinate and coordinate clauses. In addition, inflection in speech and grammatical structure become more adult. Considering the complexity of the rules of structure and usage, children's early mastery of them is astonishing.

Effects of Environment. Although favorable environmental conditions promote the development of early speech and unstimulating circumstances may retard it, social influences may have even more marked effects during the preschool period. For example, orphans adopted into foster homes are more advanced in all aspects of language development (vocabulary, articulation, sentence length, complexity and organization of language) than those living in unstimulating orphanage environments. Furthermore, these effects appear to be enduring. One longitudinal study showed that spending the first three years of life in an orphanage may result in a restriction of verbal ability that is not likely to be overcome even after a period of ordinary schooling, family life, and community experience.

On the average, twins progress more slowly than other children in all aspects of speech. This is presumably due to the twins' social situations. Since they play together and "talk" to each other a great deal, often imitating each other's speech rather than learning from adults, many of their social needs are satisfied without the usual types of verbal communication. Still, the preschool differences between the language skills of twins and single (nontwin) children, disappear surprisingly soon—within a half year—after they enter kindergarten. This finding suggests that the widening social contacts with other children and with school have an almost immediate effect on twins' motivation to learn, and their consequent acquisition of, language skills.

Furthermore, only children tend to be more advanced in verbal capacities than children from larger families. This, too, may be due to social stimulation, for an only child generally has more contacts with adults and adult speech, a wider variety of learning experiences, and more opportunities—and rewards—for practicing language.

Social-class differences in language ability have shown up consistently in many studies. Children from middle-class homes have better vocabularies, articulate more accurately, speak more correctly and grammatically, and construct more elaborate sentences than do children from lower-class homes. These differences are even more striking than the social-class differences in scores on standard intelligence tests. According to the data of one study, three-year-old children whose fathers are in the professions use more than twice as many words per sentence, on the average, as the children of unskilled laborers.

Compared with lower-class children, those of the middle and upper classes talk more with their parents, become more interested in language, and are rewarded more for verbal accomplishments. In short, language and verbal skills are more highly valued in the middle and upper classes than in the lower. Hence, it seems probable that the former are more encouraged than the latter to talk and more likely to be rewarded for demonstrating their conversational and language abilities.

The results of an interesting experiment by Professor Orvis Irwin of the University of Iowa indicate that increasing the stimulation of the environment of a young child of lower-class background will lead to heightened interest in language and improvements in speech.

Irwin secured the cooperation of a large group of mothers whose husbands were mostly skilled, semiskilled, and unskilled laborers. Ordinarily, such mothers do little reading to their children at any age, and almost certainly none in the first year or so of their babies' lives. Irwin persuaded 55 mothers to read aloud to their children for at least ten minutes a day from the time they were little more than babies (one year old). The participation in the study of another, control group of mothers was elicited by offers to check on the development of their babies. Otherwise no change was made in the interaction between them and their children.

Irwin measured the youngsters' speech development regularly and found great differences in all phases of speech by the time the children were 20 months of age. These differences appear to be highly significant statistically. . . . The study is especially provocative when we consider the relations that have been found between speech and intelligence. Irwin reports the experimental mothers' amazement and chagrined amusement: "You asked us to read ten minutes a day," many exclaimed, "but I can't get away from that kid. He wants me to read to him all the time." *

Language and Behavior

Some significant relationships between language and learning and other aspects of cognitive functioning were summarized in the last section (see pages 36–39). Children learn simple discriminations (differential responses to different stimuli) more easily if they attach names or labels to the stimuli, thus making them more distinctive. Complex learning and concept formation are even more dependent on language.

As a child's language skills improve, his behavior becomes increasingly controlled and regulated by the words of others or by instructions he gives himself. This has been demonstrated most clearly in the research of several Soviet psychologists, A. R. Luria and his colleagues, who regard language as "the essential means whereby the child finds his bearings in the external world." Their observations indicate that language functions primarily as a means of communication at the outset, but gradually becomes the most important mediator and regulator of behavior. The child's own internal speech becomes the most important source of verbal stimulation late in the preschool, or early in the school, period.

Systematic observations of the influence of language on motor learning show that adults' verbal instructions have no apparent effect on the motor behavior of infants only a few months of age. By the age of one or two, however, the child makes orienting and investigatory responses to an adult's speech. Verbal instructions to a three- or four-year-old can be effective in releasing action the child is already set to perform, or in initiating some new actions, but they cannot inhibit an action once started or switch the child from one action to another.

The language of the three- or four-year-old child is much more highly developed, richer, and more fluent. An adult's words can direct the attention of a child of this age to the distinctive features of a task or instruct him to delay action until he receives certain signals. The child of this age can carry out rather complicated instructions given by adults and he begins to regulate his activities on the basis of self-instruction. As the regulatory function of speech becomes further developed, it shifts from overt to covert, or primarily internal. This shift occurs between the ages of four-and-a-half and five-and-a-half. Luria describes the process thus:

> . . . the child's speech, which directs his solution of a problem, is at first unabbreviated and full; but . . . later, as he masters his actions, it becomes increasingly abbreviated and contracted. First, the child ceases to say everything aloud and in full; his speech sinks to a whisper, its grammatical structure becomes contracted and broken, he begins to utter only separate words indicating necessary objects or

* McCandless, B. R. *Children and adolescents—behavior and development.* New York: Holt, Rinehart and Winston, 1961, p. 260.

actions at critical points; after a certain time his speech ceases, and he begins to perform his task in silence. Occasionally, when children utter stray remarks, the fact that speech has not disappeared, but has only taken new concealed forms, is revealed. Full, overt speech, therefore, gradually becomes transformed into contracted, internal speech. This internal speech, however, continues to fulfil the same function, that of mobilizing the systematized connections of past experience, which may be useful for orientation in the new conditions and for the regulation of future actions. The child's speech, in this contracted form, is indissolubly linked with his thinking, and continues to share in those forms of activity which the child now performs in silence.*

From the age of five-and-a-half, almost all new learning involves language. According to the Russian research reports, behavior that is learned with the use of language is acquired quickly, is highly stable, and generalizes widely, whereas reactions learned without verbal participation are relatively unstable, depend on constant reinforcement, and are easily forgotten. Children over five years of age function and control their behavior primarily by means of verbal stimulation; that is, by means of what American psychologists call mediated generalization or verbal mediation.

THE DEVELOPMENT OF INTELLIGENCE

Although the definitions of intelligence are diverse, most of them stress the ability to think in abstract terms and to reason and the ability to use these functions for *adaptive* purposes. If we accept this definition, as most psychologists do, it is obviously difficult to separate intelligence and other cognitive functions. Almost all tests of intelligence contain items of perceptual discrimination, problem solving, reasoning, and abstract thinking. The relationship between verbal ability and measured intelligence is perhaps the most striking: All useful, valid intelligence tests are highly correlated with, and probably depend on, facility in language. Indeed, all aspects of language ability tend to be positively correlated with scores in intelligence tests. The latter are usually expressed in terms of IQ, which is the ratio between mental age, measured by an intelligence test, and chronolgical age multiplied by 100.

It is difficult to test the language ability or intellectual competence of infants, for these qualities are not well developed in the earliest years. Yet, because of the need for objective evaluations of very young children—for purposes of adoption, placement in foster homes, or early diagnosis of mental retardation or neurological deficiency—a number of infant intelligence tests, or schedules, have been devised. These consist primarily of sensorimotor items, and they measure what has been called "sensorimotor alertness."

Table 3 lists 22 items from one of these schedules, the California Preschool

* Luria, A. R. "The role of language in the formation of temporary connections," in Simon, B. (ed.). *Psychology in the Soviet Union.* Stanford: Stanford University Press, 1957, p. 116.

Mental Scale, which contains a total of 185 items arranged in increasing order of difficulty. This "mental series includes tests of adaptability or learning and tests or sensory acuity and fine motor (manual) coordinations." * The age placement in months of each item—that is, the age at which the average child exhibits the behavior or can accomplish the task listed—is given in the third column. Other infant intelligence tests are Cattell's Intelligence Scale for Infants and Young Children, the Merrill-Palmer Scale, the Minnesota Preschool Scale, and the Gesell Development Schedules.

TABLE 3

Items from Bayley's Mental Scale (Listed in Order of Difficulty, with Age Placement in Months)

Item No.	*Name of Test*	*Age Placement (Months)*
1	Postural adjustment when lifted	0.5
8	Arm and leg thrusts in play	1.3
15	Eyes follow pencil	2.3
23	Carries ring to mouth	3.3
30	Inspects hand	3.7
38	Picks up cube	5.2
48	Vocalizes pleasure	5.9
53	Picks cube deftly	6.2
57	Unilateral reaching	6.5
63	Smiles at image	7.2
67	Pulls string: secures ring	7.4
75	Cooperates in games	8.5
78	Says "da-da" or equivalent	8.6
83	Pulls string adaptively	9.5
91	Holds crayon adaptively	11.2
95	Imitates words	11.7
100	Dangles ring by string	13.1
103	Tower of 2 cubes	13.5
108	Throws a ball	15.8
110	Turns pages	16.6
113	Two round blocks in formboard	17.2
118	Imitates a stroke	17.8

From Mental growth during the first three years. A developmental study of sixty-one children by repeated tests. *Genet. Psychol. Monogr.*, 1933, Vol. 14, No. 1, 92 pp.

Unfortunately, these tests have very limited value. They are useful in helping to diagnose gross mental deficiency, neurological defect, and specific disabilities in social responsiveness, vision, language, and hearing in young children. But they *cannot* predict a child's later intelligence; scores on these

* Bayley, N. Mental growth during the first three years. In Barker, R. G., Kounin, J. S., and Wright, H. F. (eds.). *Child behavior and development.* New York: McGraw-Hill, 1943, p. 90.

so-called intelligence tests given before 18 months are absolutely worthless for the prediction of children's intellectual abilities when they are of school age.

Why is there no correlation between the abilities measured by these infant tests and later intelligence? Most significantly, vastly different kinds of abilities are tapped at different ages. As a child's language becomes more highly developed and as his cognitive abilities improve, items evaluating these functions predominate in the tests, replacing the sensorimotor items of the infant scales. Items at the two- and three-year levels require more verbal ability and comprehension than the earlier tests, which test motor and sensory abilities almost exclusively.

In the Stanford-Binet intelligence test, a widely used test for children, items are arranged according to the age levels at which the average child can pass them. Succeeding age levels throughout the preschool and school period include increased numbers of verbal items, more problem solving, reasoning, and abstract problems. To illustrate, the two-year-level items of this test include: identifying common objects, such as a cup, by their use; identifying major body parts; repeating two spoken digits; and placing simple blocks in a formboard. Among the four-year items are: naming pictures of a variety of common objects; recalling nine- and ten-word sentences; and correctly completing analogies (for instance, "in daytime it is light; at night it is . . .). Completing a drawing of a man, copying a square, defining simple words, and counting four objects are five-year-level tasks. The eight-year-old tests involve: comprehending, and answering questions about, a short story; recognizing absurdities in stories; defining similarities and differences in pairs of objects (for example, a penny and a quarter); and general comprehension (What makes a sail boat move?) In short, as the tests show, as a child grows older, he can master problems of increasing difficulty, which require of him greater verbal facility, comprehension, and problem-solving ability.

The predictive efficiency of test scores increases as a child matures. Table 4 reports the correlation coefficients, based on a longitudinal study of 252 children, between intelligence test scores at various ages and at 10 and at 18 years (which is young adulthood). Test scores for children below 18 months are not significantly correlated with adult intelligence, as we mentioned above, but the correlations between childhood and adult intelligence, as tested by these tests, improves as children grow older. As the table shows, IQ at the age of six or seven is relatively highly correlated with intelligence at 18. Nevertheless, according to the data of one study, almost 60 per cent of children change 20 or more points in IQ between the ages of 6 and 18, some improving rather consistently and some decreasing in IQ as they become older. We shall discuss factors related to such changes below.

Still, scores on intelligence tests taken during early school years are good predictors of grammar school grades in reading, arithmetic, composition, spelling, and social studies, and they are also fairly good predictors of success in high school, college, and various occupations.

TABLE 4

Correlations Between IQ during the Preschool and School Years and at Ages 10 and 18

Ages	*Correlation with IQ at Age 10*	*Correlation with IQ at Age 18*
2	.37	.31
3	.36	.35
4	.66	.42
6	.76	.61
7	.78	.71
8	.88	.70
9	.90	.76
10	—	.70
12	.87	.76

After Honzik, M. P., Macfarlane, J. W., and Allen, L. The stability of mental test performance between two and eighteen years. *J. Exp. Educ.*, 1948, 17,309–324.

Factors Related to Performance on Intelligence Tests

Intelligence tests do not yield "pure" measures of native ability or intellectual capacity; they measure and evaluate *performance* in specific tasks, mostly, though not entirely, of a verbal kind. This performance can be influenced by most of the factors that shape psychological development. Genetic and environmental influences produce marked effects on intelligence, as measured by tests, but it is not meaningful to ask what relative proportions of an individual's intelligence are attributable to the two sets of factors. In the determination of intelligence, heredity and environment interact in ways that make their impacts inextricable.

The Influence of Heredity on Intelligence. Two types of studies have established the effects of genetic components on intelligence. In one, the researcher compares the intelligence test scores of identical twins (who have the same heredity), reared in different environments and so exposed to different experiences, with those of fraternal twins (who have different genetic make-up) living together and presumably having similar environmental experiences. In one study, the intelligence test scores of 19 pairs of identical twins were highly correlated (+.76), whereas the scores of the fraternal twins were less highly correlated (+.63). In other words, despite being reared in vastly different environments, identical twins were more alike in intelligence, as tested, than fraternal twins who had been raised in the same environment. Obviously, heredity must be a major determinant of intelligence. Even among the identical twins, however, environmental variables had significant impacts.

The greater the differences in their environmental experiences, the more divergent were the identical twins' IQ's. For example, one of a pair of girl identical twins spent a considerable part of her elementary school years in an isolated mountain setting where there were no schools. She dropped out of school entirely when very young. Her twin sister, adopted into a home where there was much emphasis on education and accomplishment, was intellectually stimulated, particularly by her foster mother. The Stanford-Binet IQ of the first girl was 92; that of the second, 116, a difference of 24 points, and the latter was almost seven years more advanced than her sister in educational age.

The second type of study of hereditary influence on intelligence compares (1) the intelligence test scores of foster children adopted in infancy with those of their foster parents and (2) the intelligence of children raised by their true parents and that of the parents. Children resemble their true fathers and mothers in intelligence-test performance to a significantly greater degree than foster children resemble their foster parents. Presumably heredity accounts for the greater similarity in the former situation, especially since the foster children were adopted very early in life. Findings such as these leave little doubt that heredity determines the limits within which environment may raise or lower a child's intelligence test score.

Environmental Impacts on Intelligence. Despite these limitations, recent studies make it clear that motivation, personality structure, language ability, and social-psychological environment also contribute significantly to intelligence. For example, anxious, fearful children have difficulty concentrating on academic and problem-solving tasks and are likely to perform poorly on intelligence tests. On the average, children of school age, particularly boys, with high scores on tests of anxiety have somewhat lower intelligence test scores than their peers who have relatively little anxiety.

Children of the upper and middle classes are consistently superior to those of the lower class in intelligence test performance, the average difference between children of the lowest and highest social classes being 20 points of IQ. We might interpret these class differences in terms of heredity—that is, perhaps the upper classes are of superior intellectual endowment and transmit this genetically to their children. On the other hand, we can cogently argue that social and cultural factors account for class differences in intelligence test performance. Some psychologists maintain that there is a kind of cultural bias in intelligence tests, the items being more familiar and more appealing to middle- than to lower-class children. Most intelligence tests are, in fact, strongly dependent on language skills, and, as we have seen, these are better developed among middle-class than among lower-class children. This discrepancy gives the middle-class children an advantage in intelligence tests, while it penalizes those from the lower class.

Moreover, middle-class children are highly motivated to achieve in school and in academic tasks, but this is not so true of lower-class children. Since intelligence test items are like academic tasks and activities, a middle-class child's motivation to do well spurs his performance in tests, while a lower-class child is less likely to work hard on his tasks.

Interestingly enough, if a lower-class child moves into a neighborhood with better educational opportunities, his IQ is apt to increase, even though his social-class status remains low. The longer a child resides in an underprivileged area, the lower his IQ will be, on the average. Clearly, inadequate learning opportunities and unstimulating environments handicap the lower-class child's performance in intelligence tests.

We can find further evidence of significant environmental impacts on intelligence in the tendency of children reared in unstimulating environments, such as orphanage institutions, to be retarded—possibly permanently—in intelligence as well as in language development. The longer the residence in an institution, the lower a child's IQ is likely to be. Presently available data do not permit of any definitive conclusion about the enduring effects of deprivation of social stimulation early in life. Some scholars maintain that it produces irreversible deleterious effects, whereas others feel that removal from an unstimulating environment or institution may overcome initial retarding effects. Nevertheless, one authority on the matter concluded that "speaking from a social-welfare point of view, enough evidence has been accumulated to indicate that group living for babies, in a baby ward where only routine care is given, is sufficiently damaging (whether temporarily or permanently) to justify recommendations against such arrangements." *

Factors Related to Change in Intelligence. Although intelligence is fairly stable and the correlation is high between performance on intelligence tests in childhood and adulthood, many persons change significantly in IQ between these two periods. These changes appear to be related to personality traits, as this case history of a subject in a longitudinal study illustrates. The boy's IQ fluctuated between 113 and 163 during his school years, the scores varying with his general state of health, psychological adjustment, and home conditions. At the age of six, when his Stanford-Binet IQ was at its lowest, he had chronic sinus, bronchial asthma, and was in bed 12 weeks. His father contracted T.B. and his mother had to go to work; these changes produced a vast reorganization at home. The school reports at this time noted that the boy was restless, sensitive, and shy. In contrast, at age ten, when he scored 163, his father had recovered and was working again after a period of unemployment, his school adjustment had improved tremendously, and he was said to manifest "marvelous concentration" at school.

A systematic study of the personality correlates in IQ changes recently completed at the Fels Research Institute in Yellow Springs, Ohio, involved 140 subjects of a longitudinal study. Comparisons were made between the 35 children showing the greatest increase in IQ between the ages of six and

* McCandless, B. R. *Children and adolescents—behavior and development,* p. 247.

ten, and the 35 with the greatest decreases during this period. In comparison with the latter, the former, it was found, were more interested in school work, studied harder, and were more strongly motivated to master intellectual problems. In general, they were more oriented toward achievement, and their mothers had encouraged them, since early childhood, to master problems of all sorts. (This effect, incidentally, was more marked for girls than for boys.) Apparently intelligence test performance is, to a marked extent, a reflection of strength of motivation for achievement and for problem mastery. We may infer that altering this motivation may increase or decrease intelligence test scores during the school years.

PIAGET'S THEORY OF COGNITIVE DEVELOPMENT

As we have seen, psychologists have extensively investigated the characteristics of children's perceptions, thinking, and concept formation at different ages—and the determinants and stability of general tested intelligence. But basic questions about the *processes* involved in intellectual functioning and in the *development* of cognition remain unanswered.

A number of theories of cognitive development have been formulated. Among these, the most systematic and comprehensive is that of Jean Piaget and his collaborators. This theory derives from four decades of extensive and intensive naturalistic and experimental observations of children's cognitive behavior. Piaget's work has been extremely stimulating and influential. Hence, although the theory is complex, we shall summarize it briefly here.

Piaget regards intelligence as a specific instance of *adaptive* behavior, of coping with the environment and organizing (and reorganizing) thought and action. Adaptation begins with the random, diffuse, mass reflexes of the neonate state and progresses, by stages, to the formal, logical reasoning of adulthood. The transitions from one stage to another are gradual and result from continuous creative activity of the child and interaction between him and his environment. At each stage, the child's knowledge and understanding of the world (his "mental structures" or "organizations," in Piaget's terms) expand. Reorganization of information and the development of new capabilities make possible more complex types of intelligent behavior, thinking, and reasoning. The reflexes of the newborn become transformed through a series of differentiations and coordinations into the logical "organizations" of adult intelligence. With development, a child becomes capable of taking into account more stimuli, and of employing more complex techniques of solving problems. "Life is a continuous creation of increasingly complex forms and the progressive adaptation of these forms to the environment."

The growth of intelligence or adaptation always involves two complementary processes, *assimilation* and *accommodation.* In assimilation, a child incorporates and utilizes stimuli from the environment, interpreting new situations in terms of familiar ones, fitting the unfamiliar into his available "organization" and reacting as he has in past situations. Accommodation occurs when environmental stimuli demand new reactions in familiar situations—that is, when learned responses are no longer adequate and the child must "accommodate" to the situation by changing his behavior.

Piaget believes that, while physical and perceptual development seem to be continuous, intellectual development progresses in step-like ways in discrete stages. The order of succession of stages is constant, although the ages at which different stages are attained may vary somewhat, depending on the child's motivation, practice, and cultural milieu. As the child moves from one stage to the next, early structures become integrated with later ones.

Piaget has not attempted to specify the *mechanisms* or *processes* of transition between stages. Yet, as we shall see, many of his observations, and many aspects of his theory, seem congruent with some of the research findings on perception and cognition discussed earlier in this chapter and may be explained in these terms. For example, in the earliest stage of cognitive development, as Piaget describes it, orienting responses and curiosity (see pages 13–14) play a critical role in adaptation. The increasing complexity of mental structures with age and the transition from one of Piaget's stages to the next may be attributable, at least in part, to activities and phenomena such as exploration, language acquisition and improvement in verbal skills, mediated generalization, and reversal learning.

The following is a highly condensed account of Piaget's theory of the major stages of cognitive development.

Stage I, Sensorimotor Operations

According to Piaget's theory, the first stage in the development of adaptive behavior, the *sensorimotor,* extends from birth to about two years of age, and is divided into six phases. For the first month, an infant only exercises the reflexes present at birth (his only mental "organizations" at this time), but the second stage, from roughly one to four months, involves *coordination of reflexes and responses.* Hand movements become coordinated with eye movements; what he hears he looks at (orienting reflex); he reaches for objects, grasps and sucks them.

In the third phase, approximately four to eight months, an infant begins to anticipate the consequences of his actions and can *intentionally* repeat responses that have produced interesting results. For example, at four months of age, a baby will kick his legs in order to make a toy suspended over his crib swing. Moreover, becoming interested in the objective world, he begins to look for objects he has lost sight of. In the fourth phase, the child begins to differentiate means from ends, using established responses to attain goals. Thus, if a desirable toy is hidden, he will actively search for it and he will remove an obstacle in order to get it. The fifth phase, beginning at 11 or 12 months of age, is characterized by active experimentation, exploration, variation, and modification of behavior. The child appears to be genuinely interested in novelty and manifests a great deal of curiosity. He drops objects to watch them fall, pulls toys toward him with strings, and uses sticks to push things around.

Between 18 months and two years of age the child is in the sixth and final phase of the sensorimotor period. This represents an important advance from the other stage, for it is characterized by the emergence of the capacity to respond to, or think about, objects and events that are not immediately observable, and to *invent* new means of accomplishing goals through "mental combinations," that is, imagination and ideas. Objects may be considered in new relationships to one another. Thus, the child may use a stick as a tool for drawing an object toward him, even though he has never used a stick in this way previously.

Some degree of problem solving, remembering, planning, imagining, and pretending are all possible at this stage, which most children have achieved by the age of two. Nevertheless, "Although genuine intelligence emerges at the sixth sensorimotor stage, the gap between the sensorimotor intelligence of the infant aged a year-and-a-half and two and the reflective intelligence of adults is wide indeed. In fact, this gap is approximately equivalent to that between the intelligence of the dog, the monkey, or the chimpanzee, and the intelligence of adult man." *

Stage II, Concrete Operations

The emergence of real symbolic activity occurs during the second broad period of intellectual development, the stage of *concrete operations,* which extends from about 18 months or two years until the ages of 11 or 12. During the first part of this period, *the preconceptual stage* (ages two to four), a child begins to regard stimuli as representatives of other objects. Imagery, or "symbolic function," develops during this stage and, at the same time, the child acquires more facility in language, and he begins to engage in symbolic play. His tricycle may be used as a racing car, a tree stump as a castle, and a twig as a machine gun.

During the next part of the stage of concrete operations, *the period of intuitive thought* (approximately age four to age seven), the child conceptualizes more, elaborates his concepts, and constructs more complex thoughts and images. Moreover, he becomes able to group objects together into classes, according to his own perceptions of similarity. This is undoubtedly due to improvement in the child's language ability, which, as we learned earlier, is of paramount importance in verbal mediation, concept formation, abstraction, and problem solving. Recall also that, according to the Russian data, children of this age instruct and direct themselves, largely by means of covert speech.

At this period, the child's concepts and his understanding of situations are

* Hunt, J. McV. *Intelligence and experience.* New York: Ronald Press, 1961, p. 170.

likely to be determined by whatever he happens to perceive, often a single, salient aspect of a particular object or event. Ordinarily he will not relate different aspects or dimensions of a situation to one another. For example, in one experiment, a child is given two equal balls of clay and asked to roll one of them into a long sausage, to flatten it into a pancake, or to break it into small pieces. Then he is asked whether the quantity of matter has increased, decreased, or remains equal. Most five- and six-year-olds think that a change in form necessarily produces a change in amount. Being able to take account of only one dimension, such as the length, at a time, a child of this age is likely to report that the sausage contains more clay than the ball because it is longer.

At about seven years of age, the youngster begins to relate different aspects or dimensions of a situation to one another and finally arrives at the notion of conservation, or what Piaget labels the "principle of invariance." In responding to the question about the amount of clay in the ball or sausage, the child is likely to reason that "If you make the sausage into a ball again you see that nothing is added and nothing is taken away." In short, he is now aware of the fact that the amount of clay remains *constant* in spite of changes in shape. Furthermore, he acquires the concept of *reversibility*—the idea that, in thought, steps can be retraced, actions can be cancelled, and the original situation can be restored. Thus, in making a sausage of a ball of clay, the diminution in the height of the ball is compensated for by the increase in length, so that the same quantity of clay is maintained. The number two can be squared to get four, and extracting the square root of four yields two. Using the concept of reversibility, the child can interrupt a sequence of steps in problem solving if he sees that he is not succeeding; and he can then return mentally to the beginning and start again.

It should be noted that this concept of reversibility is related to reversal learning which, as we have seen, depends on abstraction and concept formation (see page 37). This kind of learning becomes easier as children grow older and, according to experimental findings, a considerable proportion of seven-year-olds can deal efficiently with reversal problems.

In the stage of concrete operations, a child uses logic and reasoning in an elementary way, but he applies them *only* in the manipulation of concrete objects, not to verbal propostions. Thus, Piaget and his colleagues found that eight- and ten-year-olds have no trouble ordering a series of dolls or sticks according to height, but they have difficulty with verbal problems such as this one: "Edith is taller than Susan; Edith is shorter than Lilly; who is the tallest of the three?"

The ability to deal with this kind of verbal expression of logical relationship requires the use of "formal operations" as distinct from "concrete operations," and the child does not ordinarily use these until the age of 11 or 12. In the view of Piaget and Inhelder, one of Piaget's chief collaborators, this ability to apply logical rules, reasoning, and "formal operations" to abstract problems and propositions is the essence of intellectual growth and ability.

Stage III, Formal Operations

The final stage of intellectual development begins early in adolescence. While in the stage of concrete operations, a child can only classify, count, and put into series the various objects and events he perceives. An adolescent in the stage of formal operations can "operate with the operations," that is, by means of symbolic propositions. A child's concrete thought operations occur in response to real situations. An adolescent can consider general laws, and his thoughts concern what is hypothetically possible as well as what is real.*

As the Soviet psychologists have pointed out, much of the preadolescent's language becomes abbreviated, contracted, and more internalized. He formulates rules and engages in a great deal of self-instruction, although he does not state his rules or instructions overtly. Extensive use of covert speech is undoubtedly related to many advances in cognitive functions during adolescence. The adolescent can reason deductively, making hypotheses about problem solutions, and keeping in mind many variables simultaneously. He is capable of scientific reasoning and of formal logic in verbal argument. Moreover, at this stage, he reflects about, evaluates, and criticizes the logic and quality of his own thinking. His dependence on the perception or manipulation of concrete objects is reduced, he need no longer confine his attention to the immediate situation. "He can consider hypotheses which may or may not be true, and consider what would follow if they were true. He can follow the form of an argument while disregarding its concrete content. It is from this last characteristic that *formal operations* get their name." †

The adolescent's ability to think scientifically is clearly illustrated by one experiment reported by Inhelder and Piaget. A subject is presented with five bottles of colorless liquid. The contents of bottles one, three, and five, when combined, produce a brownish color; the fourth contains a color-reducing solution; and the second is neutral. The problem is to produce the brown solution. Adolescents in the stage of formal operations discover the solution little by little, by combining the various possibilities logically, and determining the effectiveness or neutrality of each liquid.

In short, an adolescent reasons scientifically, forming hypotheses and testing them in reality or in thought. Although a younger child's thought involves only concrete objects, the adolescent can imagine what might be possible. He can speculate and his speculations are governed by logical rules. By the time he is 15, the adolescent is able to use logical operations and formal logic in an adult manner in solving problems. He has, according to Inhelder and Piaget, reached the critical stage in intellectual development.

* This discussion is based on J. McV. Hunt's *Intelligence and experience.*
† *Ibid.,* p. 230.

The Development of Personality

Personality is a broad and comprehensive concept covering the organization of an individual's predispositions to behavior and his unique adjustments to his environment. Personal characteristics (or traits), emotions, motivations, values, goals, and ways of perceiving are all aspects of personality structure.

Personality development is an enormously complicated process, influenced by a vast number of interrelated and continually interacting factors. At least four broad types of influence play a role in determining a child's characteristics and behavior. The first is *biological properties,* such as genetic endowment, temperament, physical ap-

5

pearance, and rate of maturation. The second is *cultural group membership*. Hopi and Zuni children, reared on Indian reservations, live in physical environments and have social experiences that are vastly different from those of other American children. Hence, they develop characteristics that are different from those of white peers. The third, and from the author's point of view, most important, factor is *the individual's personal history of experiences with others*. Personality is largely a product of social learning, and a child's social interactions provide the crucial learning situations. Relationships with family, with other members of social-class, ethnic, and religious groups, and with teachers and peers are of outstanding significance. The fourth type of influence on overt behavior and personality characteristics is the *situation*, that is, the stimuli immediately present in the environment, such as other people who are present, and the feelings of the moment (for instance, fatigue, frustration, anxiety, calm, relaxation).

All these forces are interwoven—operating, interacting, and affecting personality development concurrently. Thus, although a child's cultural group membership and his relationships with his parents are central in shaping his personality and behavior, their effects may be conditioned by his energy and activity levels, which are, at least partially, biologically determined.

It is only for convenience of exposition that in the following discussion of personality development we focus on important biological and social forces one at a time. In actuality, it is often difficult to separate the effects of one determinant from those of another. Moreover, our knowledge is still very much limited. The solutions to many problems in personality development—such as the relative impacts of various biological, social, and situational factors—await further scientific research.

BIOLOGICAL FACTORS

By and large, the influences of biological factors on personality structure are limited and indirect. Genetic, hereditary factors; physical appearance and physique; and rate of maturation—all of these biological variables have some impact.

Genetic Inflences on Personality and Behavior

It is impossible to separate the relative contributions of heredity and environment in shaping human characteristics, since heredity always interacts with environment and learning.

> The old problem of "heredity *or* environment" is essentially meaningless. The two sets of determinants can rarely be completely disentangled once the environment has begun to operate. All geneticists are agreed today that traits are not inherited in any simple sense. The observed characteristics of organisms are, at any given point in time, the product of a long series of complex interactions between biologically inherited potentialities and environmental forces. The outcome of each

interaction is a modification of the personality. The only pertinent questions therefore are: (1) which of the various genetic potentialities will be actualized as a consequence of a particular series of life-events in a given physical, social, and cultural environment? and (2) what limits to the development of this personality are set by genetic constitution? *

There is clear-cut evidence that certain characteristics of dogs and other animals—such as aggressiveness, nervousness, timidity and sociability—are strongly influenced by genetic endowment. For example, selective breeding can produce litters of mild, calm dogs or of nervous, aggressive ones. There is no evidence that such characteristics are transmitted genetically in human beings, however. Undoubtedly, though, an individual's constitutional make-up (which is largely determined by heredity) influences his personality development in indirect ways. Thus, neonates can be reliably classified as unusually active, moderately active, or quiet, these differences being attributable primarily to heredity. Infants' activity patterns remain relatively stable for the first few years, although environment and culture may produce modifications.

In general, an active, energetic infant explores more vigorously and exposes himself to more situations and to a wider environment than a quiet, passive one. Moreover, the reactions he elicits from others will be different from those elicited by a more quiet child. Of course, the effects of an infant's activity level will depend upon his family's attitudes. An exuberant, accepting family may welcome and encourage noisy activity and energetic responses in its newest member, whereas more restrictive parents may consider such activity irritating or frightening, and so suppress the child's "natural" active tendencies. In sum, a child's activity level may not influence his subsequent personality development directly, but the associated experiences may. A child's activity level affects his social learning because it systematically affects the behavior of people who come in contact with him.

Influences of Physical Appearance and Physique

As we noted earlier in this volume, physical appearance—structure of the face, height, weight, body proportions—is to a large extent genetically determined. Casual observation, to say nothing of biography and fiction, attests that physical appearance and physique may significantly affect personality and behavior. Everyone is acquainted with someone who, because of ugliness or deformity, became profoundly unhappy, shy, or even extremely withdrawn. A handsome, well-built ten-year-old boy will probably enjoy greater social prestige and acceptance by peers than a boy who is slight, weak, and unattractive. As a result, the former is more likely to become a self-confident, outgoing, and socially successful individual.

Obviously these effects may be exaggerated or mitigated by other factors

* Kluckhohn, C., Murray, H. A., and Schneider, D. M. (eds.). *Personality in nature, society, and culture.* New York: Knopf, 1953, p. 56.

in a child's life. The tall, well-built, good-looking boy is not likely to become secure and self-confident if he happens to be unintelligent and unsuccessful in school or if, as a result of his relationships at home, he is insecure and dependent. On the other hand, if the weak, unattractive boy is bright and academically successful, or has stable, reassuring relationships at home, he may not become insecure in spite of the fact that his physical appearance initially arouses unfavorable reactions from his peers.

Cultural pressures may modify the effects of genetic endowments. For example, many white American and Zuni neonates can be reliably classified as "unusually active," presumably as a result of heredity. By the age of two, however, the Zuni child who was classified this way may seem unusually lively in comparison with other Zuni children but he will not be as quick, active, and restless as his white peer. What happens is that early in life, Zunis learn to reduce or inhibit tendencies (presumably genetically determined) toward intense, vigorous activity.

Systematic studies of normal children show that there are small, but significant, relationships between body build and personality. According to the data of one study of ten- and eleven-year-olds, small, poorly coordinated, and relatively weak children are inclined to be timid, fearful, passive, and generally worried. In contrast, tall, strong, energetic, well-coordinated children of the same age are playful, self-expressive, talkative, productive, and creative. It hardly seems likely that constitutional factors influence these personality characteristics directly. Rather, some features of physique may affect an individual's capabilities, aptitudes, and interests. And, perhaps even more critically, a child's physical characteristics tend to arouse certain expectancies in others and influence their reactions to him, and, in this indirect way, play a role in molding his personality.

To illustrate, in our culture, people are likely to expect small, awkward, physically weak children to be delicate, sensitive, dependent, relatively unaggressive, and perhaps lacking in competence. Furthermore, because of their physical limitations, such children are not likely to be proficient in motor activities and athletics and, consequently, they may be somewhat rejected by their peers. For these reasons, they may learn to withdraw from others, as well as from physical activities, and, not surprisingly, they may become timid, passive, and dependent.

Tall, strong, heavy, well-coordinated children, on the other hand, may be expected to be independent, aggressive, competent, and mature, and others are likely to react to them as though they actually possessed these characteristics. In addition, these children are likely to be skillful in motor activities, successful in athletics, and energetic in social interactions. For these reasons, they may be accorded high social status, and may therefore develop self-confidence and outgoing characteristics. They are more likely to feel free to express themselves and to propose original, creative ideas in a relatively uninhibited way. In sum, a child's physical characteristics may be related to his approach to the social environment, to the expectancies of others, and to their reactions to him. These, in turn, may have impacts on personality development.

Rate of Maturing

As we learned earlier, there are striking variations in the ages at which adolescents reach physical maturity. The relatively mature and immature adolescents of the same age are undoubtedly exposed to different social-psychological environments. A late-maturing boy looks younger than his age and is likely to be regarded and treated as immature by others, while the early-maturing boy is likely to be credited with being more grown up socially and emotionally. In addition, the latter has an advantage over the former in the competitive athletic activities that are so important during adolescence.

The psychological consequences of these differences have been demonstrated in studies comparing the personalities of late- and early-maturing adolescent boys. Those who are relatively retarded physically tend to reveal more maladjustment than the other group. They make more negative evaluations of themselves, harbor stronger feelings of inadequacy and rejection, and are both more dependent and more rebellious. In contrast, the early-maturing boys generally feel adequate, accepted by others, self-confident, independent, mature, and capable of playing an adult role. Apparently these boys are more likely than the others to live in circumstances that are conducive to good psychological adjustment.

We must interpret these findings cautiously, however, for

> . . . although rate of maturing and associated factors may affect personality development, the relationship between physical status and psychological characteristics is by no means simple. A vast number of complex, interacting factors, including rate of maturation, determine each adolescent's unique personality structure. Hence, in any specific instance, the *group* findings . . . may not be directly applicable, for other physical, psychological, or social factors may attenuate the effects of late- or early-maturing. For example, an adolescent boy who is fundamentally secure and has warm, accepting parents and generally rewarding social relationships may not develop strong feelings of inadequacy even if he matures slowly. Analogously, the early-maturing boy who has deep feelings of insecurity, for whatever reasons, will probably not gain self-confidence simply because he matures early. In summary, in understanding any individual case, generalizations based on [these] data . . . must be particularized in the light of the individual's past history and present circumstances.*

CULTURAL DETERMINANTS OF PERSONALITY

From the point of view of personality development, the most significant aspect of a child's world is his *social* environment. Virtually all human beings live in a society, an interacting group of people. And each society has a

* Mussen, P. H., and Jones, M. C. Self-conceptions, motivations, and interpersonal attitudes of late- and early-maturing boys. *Child Development,* June, 1957, 28, 255.

distinctive culture, a body of stored knowledge, characteristic ways of thinking and feeling, attitudes, goals, and ideals.

"Culture regulates our lives at every turn. From the moment we are born until we die there is, whether we are conscious of it or not, constant pressure upon us to follow certain types of behavior that other men have created for us." * An individual's biological heritage is directly or indirectly influential in the development of his personality, but cultural factors play an overriding role, as the following story—told by the late Clyde Kluckhohn, famous Harvard anthropologist—illustrates:

> Some years ago I met in New York City a young man who did not speak a word of English and was obviously bewildered by American ways. By "blood" he was as American as you or I, for his parents had gone from Indiana to China as missionaries. Orphaned in infancy, he was reared by a Chinese family in a remote village. All who met him found him more Chinese than American. The facts of his blue eyes and light hair were less impressive than a Chinese style of gait, Chinese arm and hand movements, Chinese facial expression, and Chinese modes of thought. The biological heritage was American, but the cultural training had been Chinese.†

How does an individual's cultural group membership influence the development of his personality? Primarily by prescribing—and limiting—what a child will be taught and what he will learn. As we shall demonstrate, each culture expects, and trains, its members to behave in the ways that are acceptable to the group. To a marked degree, the child's cultural group defines the range of experiences and situations he is likely to encounter, and the values and personality characteristics that will be reinforced and hence learned. Each culture has its own concepts and specific techniques of child rearing, as well as a set of expectations regarding patterns of approved behavior.

Cultural Variations

All cultures must cope with certain universal problems and events. Every culture makes provisions for perpetuating the group and maintaining its solidarity, for establishing an orderly way of life, and for satisfying the biological needs of its members. In all cultures, children must be fed, toilet-trained, protected from illness, taught to control sexual and aggressive impulses, and liberated from dependence on their parents. Cultural variations in the methods of achieving these goals are numberless, however. The cultural prescriptions for child rearing in some cultures call for gentle handling of an infant together with prompt and complete attention to all his needs, whereas other cultures advocate rather severely frustrating treatment of infant and young child. We can demonstrate cultural contrasts in specific training procedures by breast-feeding: few

* Kluckhohn, C. *Mirror for man.* New York: McGraw-Hill, 1949, p. 327.
† *Ibid.,* pp. 320–321.

American babies are breast-fed for more than a few months but, in some cultures, infants may be permitted to nurse until they are five or six years old. Similarly, babies in some cultures are toilet-trained gradually and with help, whereas in others they are expected to achieve bladder and bowel control by the age of six months and are punished if they have accidents after that time. Early attitudes toward an infant and specific techniques of handling him may have impact on his later personality, attitudes, and social orientations (see pages 66–70); therefore, cultural differences in child-rearing practices may produce different "culturally normal" (normal for a particular culture) personality structures.

> Puberty is a biological fact. But one culture ignores it, another prescribes in formal instruction about sex but no ceremony, a third has impressive rites for girls only, a fourth for boys and girls. In this culture, the first menstruation is welcomed as a happy natural event; in that culture the atmosphere is full of dread and supernatural threat.*

In some societies, such as our own, the transition from childhood to adulthood is relatively abrupt and difficult. American culture demands that, within a relatively short period of time, an adolescent solve many problems—achieving some independence from his family; choosing and preparing for a vocation; and making a mature, heterosexual adjustment, including marriage and the setting-up of a separate household. Cultural pressures require him rapidly to learn many new and difficult responses, even though he may wish to remain secure, dependent, and free of responsibility. Under these circumstances, it is to be expected that, in America, adolescence is often a period of stress, conflict, and emotional upset.

In other societies, an adolescent receives more gradual preparation for independence, for his vocational role, and for mature sexuality. Among certain American Indian tribes, for example, training for adult vocations begins early as a child participates in the work of the community, doing menial tasks first and assuming more important responsibilities as he matures. In cultures such as this, adolescence is not a period of much stress and conflict and adolescents are likely to have fewer problems.

Analogously, in many cultures, children and adolescents are permitted considerable sexual license, and they may indulge quite freely in sex play and experimentation. Children in these societies do not learn to inhibit their sexual impulses, and, as adults, they are much less prone to sexual conflicts and problems. In sharp contrast, the American middle-class child learns early in life that sexual feelings and activities must be inhibited, and he is taught to be anxious about them. Yet he is expected to have satisfying sexual relations, without anxiety, after he is married. It hardly seems surprising that strong conflicts about sex are relatively common in our culture.

* *Ibid.*, p. 326.

Culture and Personality

Every culture prizes—and rewards the acquisition of—its own particular approved pattern of traits, motives, values, and ways of thinking. But these patterns vary widely from culture to culture. In American culture, for instance, children are encouraged to learn self-reliance and independence—together with the denial of dependent feelings. Failure to act independently or self-reliantly, or asking for help, may provoke anxiety or feelings of inadequacy in American children and adolescents. In traditional Chinese culture, on the other hand, independence is not so highly prized, and asking for help is not so likely to produce feelings of inferiority.

General American culture—middle-class American culture in particular—stresses competition and personal achievement. Early in life, American children are made aware of the value of accomplishment, and, as they grow older, rewards for competition increase and competitive attitudes become stronger. In contrast, sharing and cooperation are stressed by the Hopis and on Israeli kibbutzim (collective farms), and children in these cultures are discouraged from competing. In American schoolrooms, competition is a powerful motive for doing good work rapidly and efficiently, while among Hopis, children who complete their work quickly are likely to "hold back," for they are reluctant to embarrass others. White Americans are likely to strive to achieve "leading" positions in school or community, but Hopi children refuse such honors, preferring to remain equal, but not superior, to their peers.

Social-Class Differences

American society is not an undifferentiated entity. Within it are a large number of ethnic and social-class groups, each with its distinct culture, philosophy of life, system of values, and ways of behaving. There are, for instance, marked class differences in child-rearing practices, although, as recent studies show, these may change over a period of time. Thus, according to surveys conducted in the early 1940's, lower-class mothers were less frustrating and more permissive with their children than those of the middle class; they breast-fed for longer periods of time and used less pressure in toilet-training. More recent evidence, however, shows that middle-class mothers have become more permissive in their practices and, in general, are now warmer and more demonstrative than the lower-class group. Children from different socioeconomic backgrounds differ in personality structure, behavior, and attitudes, and these differences may be in part attributable to variations in child-rearing techniques.

The values associated with class and ethnic groups are reflected in children's motivations, personality characteristics, and attitudes. For example, middle-class children are likely to inhibit the expression of aggressive feelings, because they have learned that, in their culture, aggression leads to punishment. Lower-class children, however, are encouraged to express aggressive feelings, and, consequently, are much more likely to fight and swear when angry. Lower-class youngsters are generally less inhibited than those of the middle class in sexual expression, too. The lower-class child's sexual interests and activities are not so likely to be punished and, during adolescence, many more lower-class children experience sexual intercourse.

Classes differ with respect to achievement motivation also: Middle-class parents in general stress achievement strongly and reward it frequently, but lower-class parents do not. Consequently, middle-class children are far more interested in studying and in earning good grades in school than are children from lower-class homes. The latter do not usually seem to be motivated to do well in school or, for that matter, in psychological tests. They are inclined to have academic difficulties, often find school boring, and are more likely to become "school problems," being troublesome to teachers and generally resistant to learning.

A middle-class child's tendency to inhibit aggression and sexual expression along with his high achievement motivation may be considered manifestations of a general middle-class emphasis on "delay of gratification," that is, on the importance of sacrificing immediate goals to obtain more substantial long-term objectives. In studies in which children must choose between the alternatives of a small, immediate reward (say, a small amount of candy) and a larger, delayed reward (say, a large candy bar the next day), lower-class children tend to choose the first alternative, whereas middle-class children prefer the second. Sociological analysis suggests that the lower-class child develops little capacity to "delay gratification" because, for him, the future is uncertain, and he is frequently frustrated in attempting to satisfy his basic needs. Since he cannot depend on future gratifications, he acts in accordance with the philosophy that "a bird in the hand is worth two in the bush."

FAMILY INFLUENCES ON PERSONALITY DEVELOPMENT

Socialization

Socialization is the process by which an individual infant acquires, from the enormously wide range of behavioral potentialities that are open to him at birth, those behavior patterns that are customary and acceptable according to the standards of his family and social group. Within the limits set by his hereditary endowments and abilities, a child can become almost any type of person: aggressive or mild; competitive or cooperative; meat-eating or vegetarian; motivated toward, or uninterested in, intellectual achievement; sexually libertine or restricted; dependent or independent; honest or dishonest. The possibilities are, in effect, almost infinite; yet ordinarily any individual adopts only the behavior deemed appropriate to his own sex, social, ethnic, and religious groups. How this occurs—how the individual acquires these, rather than other, characteristics—is the core problem in studying the process of socialization.

Social Learning in the Family

You may infer from our discussion in the last section that socialization is determined to a considerable degree by *cultural prescription*, that is, an individual's culture delineates the personality characteristics, motives, attitudes, and values he will adopt. But these cultural prescriptions must be communicated or taught to the child, initially, by members of his family, the representatives of the culture with whom he is most intimate.

Thus, a child's first social learning occurs at home, and his earliest experiences with his family, particularly with his mother, are critical in determining his attitude toward, and his expectations of, other individuals.

Typically, the mother gratifies the infant's primary needs for food, for alleviation of pain, for warmth, and perhaps even for tactile stimulation (which may be a basic, innate drive). Many of these satisfactions are provided as she feeds the baby. In addition, she helps relieve his pain and supplies warmth when he needs it. For these reasons, the mother's presence—the visual, auditory, and tactile stimuli she presents—becomes associated with the satisfaction of needs, and she begins to stand for pleasure, relief of tension, and contentment. Furthermore, the infant soon learns to search for and approach his mother whenever he is hungry, in pain, or uncomfortable. If the mother is nurturant and gratifies his needs promptly and effectively, she rewards the child's "approach" responses and these are likely to be repeated.

Positive, approach responses to the mother, if frequently and strongly rewarded, will generalize to other people as well (principle of stimulus generalization). That is, the child will develop favorable social attitudes, approaching others when he needs help and generally responding to others in a friendly and outgoing manner. In this sense, the child's interactions with his mother form the bases for his reactions toward others.

> But what of the situation in which the initial feeding experience is not rewarding—a situation in which pain may be associated with the act of feeding, or where tactile contact is held to a minimum? If a mother is anxious and tense she is apt to hold her baby in an awkward way, perhaps making the child uncomfortable. If the mother did not want the child, she might resent the labor and bother involved in caring for him. This resentment might be manifested in rough handling of the infant, in stopping the feeding before the child is gratified, or, in some cases, letting the child cry for a long time before feeding him. In these instances, the child will experience both pleasure and pain in association with the cues of the mother and the stimulus of hunger. If the painful stimuli occur frequently enough, and over a long enough period of time, the cue of the mother may acquire a negative value and she will become symbolic of pain rather than of pleasure. Since an organism's innate reaction to pain is withdrawal and avoidance, the infant may learn the response of avoiding rather than approaching his mother. Moreover, he is not likely to learn that to approach people when in a state of discomfort is one way of gratifying needs. Another infant, for whom the feeding experience has been predominantly pleasant, will be more likely to look to others for gratification of his needs.*

* Mussen, P. H., Conger, J. J., and Kagan, J. S. *Child development and personality.* New York: Harper & Row, 1963, p. 158.

According to Erik Erikson, a Harvard University psychoanalyst, these earliest interactions between a mother and her infant lay the groundwork for the child's development of a sense of trust or distrust in the world. Rewarding and gratifying experiences with his mother lead the infant to trust her and, by generalization, to trust *others*. In contrast, a mother who is not dependable or does not minister to the child's needs satisfactorily, produces a sense of distrust of her, and by generalization, of the world.

> Experiences connected with feeding are a prime source for the development of trust. At around four months of age a hungry baby will grow quiet and show signs of pleasure at the sound of an approaching footstep, anticipating (trusting) that he will be held and fed. This repeated experience of being hungry, seeing food, receiving food, and feeling relieved and comforted assures the baby that the world is a dependable place.*

Gross neglect, abuse, and extreme deprivation of affection in early infancy may result in temporary, or even enduring, maladjustments. Thus, infants reared in emotionally cold and unstimulating environments—for example, institutions, where they are cared for routinely and without individual attention—tend to be quiet, passive, inactive, unhappy, and emotionally disturbed.

> The outstanding features [they present] are listlessness, emaciation, and pallor, relative immobility, quietness, unresponsiveness to stimuli like a smile or a coo, indifferent appetite, failure to gain weight properly despite ingestion of diets which are entirely adequate, frequent stools, poor sleep, an appearance of unhappiness, proneness to febrile episodes, absence of sucking habits.†

Moreover, among infants between 6 and 12 months of age, separation from mother often results in "an emotional tone of apprehension and sadness, . . . withdrawal from the environment amounting to rejection of it, . . . and no attempt to contact strangers and no brightening if a stranger contacts him. Activities are retarded and the child often sits or lies inert in a dazed stupor. Insomnia is common and lack of appetite universal. Weight is lost and the child becomes prone to . . . infections."** The reinstitution of favorable, satisfying mother-child relationships can lead to a resumption of the normal course of behavior development and the disappearance of emotionally maladaptive behavior, but only if the period of deprivation is not too long, specifically, less than six months.

In one study, infant orphans reared in a deprived, psychologically inadequate institution were moved to a much more stimulating setting where they received individual attention, were talked to, played with, and allowed to play with toys. Improvements in mental alertness and intelligence were

* The course of healthy personality development. Midcentury White House Conference on Children and Youth. In Seidman, J. M. (ed.). *The adolescent—a book of readings.* New York: Holt, Rinehart and Winston, 1960, p. 219.

† Bakwin, H. Emotional deprivation in infants. *J. Pediatrics,* 1949, 35,512–529, in *ibid.,* p. 220.

** Spitz, R., in *ibid.,* p. 220.

striking, the average gain in intelligence score being 27 points. A control group of children, who remained in the unstimulating institution, showed an average decline of 16 points during the same period.

Other consequences of emotionally inadequate rearing of infants were demonstrated in a study conducted in Iran. Infants in a *deprived* orphanage—where they were handled impersonally, had no toys, and little opportunity to practice motor activities—were compared with a group in an *enriched* orphanage where they received more personal attention, had more toys, and enjoyed greater opportunities for motor practice. The children in the enriched orphanage were considerably more content, emotionally more mature, and happier than the others and, during their second year, were more advanced in motor ability.

In addition to these observational studies, two fascinating experimental studies also shed some light on the effects of different kinds of maternal treatment on the behavior of infants. In the first, Professor Harry Harlow of the University of Wisconsin used monkeys as subjects in testing the effects of the mother's touch on infant behavior. He put newly born monkeys with "mothers" made of wire mesh (see Figure 5). Some were fed from a bottle attached to the chest of an unadorned wire "mother," while the "mother" of the others was made of wire mesh, but covered with terry cloth material. The latter structure thus supplied both food and a great deal of tactile stimulation whereas the former gave food, but not the same quantity or quality of

Figure 5. One of Harlow's monkeys with both a terry cloth and a wire-mesh mother. Even if fed by the wire mesh mother, the animal goes to the cloth mother when he is frightened. (Courtesy Harry Harlow, Primate Laboratory, The University of Wisconsin. Photograph by Robert Sponholz.)

tactile stimulation. Given the choice of going to either "mother," baby monkeys characteristically preferred the terry cloth one and spent more time clinging to her than to the other one, even those babies originally fed by the plain wire-mesh mother. When a frightening, wooden spider was placed in the cage with a young monkey, he would run to the terry cloth mother, who apparently was the more effective source of security, even if he had been raised on a lactating wire mother. The experimenter concluded that tactile stimulation is innately satisfying to an infant animal, so he forms a strong attachment to whatever or whoever offers it.

In another study, the amount of mothering given to 16 babies in an orphanage was experimentally manipulated. Eight infants, the experimental group, received a great deal of individual attention for a period of eight weeks. During this period, the experimenter mothered them for eight hours a day, five days a week, taking care of them, performing all necessary functions calmly and warmly, bathing and diapering them, playing with them, smiling and talking to them. The other eight infants, the control group, were handled in an impersonal, institutional way, several women attending to their needs in a more routine, though kindly, manner.

The reactions of the two groups differed strikingly following the experimental period. The infants in the experimental group learned positive social responses to their nurturing, stimulating mother, and these generalized to other people. When the experimenter-mother, or examiners, or strangers smiled at, or talked to, them, the infants reacted in friendly, outgoing ways or smiled back. The controls, who had experienced only routine institutional attention, seldom manifested as much social responsiveness when approached by adults. Since the period of individualized mothering was brief, the effects were not enduring. The results nevertheless demonstrate that, as a result of warm, attentive, mothering, an infant develops socially outgoing responses, whereas routine, impersonal care may inhibit the development of this behavior.

Enduring Effects. There is some evidence that, as many theorists maintain, early mother-child relationships influence not only a child's immediate behavior, but also his subsequent, long-term adjustment. The exact nature and extent of the enduring consequences of early child-rearing practices have not been clearly established, so we must interpret the results of studies of these effects cautiously.

As we learned in Chapter 4, children brought up in institutions are likely to be retarded in language development for a long time (see page 43), and there may be other persisting effects of early institutionalization. One investigator, William Goldfarb, compared the later development of two groups of orphans reared in different settings during their first three years. The children in one group were adopted into foster homes as young infants, and presumably had more individual attention, nurturance, warmth, and adequate mothering. The other group remained for three years in an institution, where they were emotionally deprived and experienced impersonal care and inadequate mothering. Many of these latter children were subsequently placed in foster homes.

The researcher studied the children longitudinally at four ages—three-and-a-half, six-and-a-half, eight-and-a-half, and twelve. He observed and interviewed them, and gave them tests of intelligence, educational achievement, personality, motor coordination, social maturity, and language ability.

The institution-reared group were relatively retarded intellectually. At all ages they performed more poorly than the foster-home children on all intelligence tests, especially in the areas of concept formation, reasoning, and abstract thinking. Language and speech difficulties were more common among the institution-reared children and persisted long after they left the orphanage.

Personality and adjustment also appeared to be affected adversely by institutional upbringing. Those reared in the orphanage were more maladjusted than the others; they lacked self-control and behaved more aggressively. They were more distractible and hyperactive, and they more frequently lied, stole, destroyed property, threw temper tantrums, and hit and kicked others. In addition, they were more dependent on adults, demanding attention frequently and asking for help unnecessarily.

Institution-reared children had not developed a basic sense of trust in others. Their social relationships were superficial and they remained emotionally withdrawn and unresponsive, avoiding strong affectionate attachments. The investigator concluded that social and emotional maladjustment, persisting into adolescence, were the results of the severe deprivations and the emotional unresponsiveness of their early environment.

In interpreting these findings, we must keep in mind that these striking effects were noted among children who were *markedly* deprived of personal, warm, maternal care in the earliest years. The consequences of lesser degrees of deprivation—that is, mildly inadequate mothering—are unknown.

Child-rearing Techniques during the Second Year

During the second year, a child acquires many new and important skills and improves on old ones. He learns to walk, his language abilities increase, and his manual skills and motor coordination progress rapidly. The two-year-old enjoys exploring—trying out his new abilities, investigating his surroundings, and testing his capacities. Parental attitudes toward the child's growing independence and their reactions to his curiosity and explorations may strongly influence the development of important motives—for example, curiosity, and the drives for autonomy, independence, mastery, competence, and achievement.

Permissive, easygoing parents will allow their child to explore and investigate freely, encouraging and rewarding his curiosity and independent behavior. As a result, their offspring are apt to continue to explore and to attempt to manipulate their environment actively, thereby developing self-confidence, spontaneity, and the desires for competence and mastery of their surroundings. Exploration means encountering new situations, trying out new responses and experimenting with new ways of doing things; in short, it brings a multiplicity of learning opportunities. A child who has tried to ride a tricycle and achieved success at it is more likely to attempt to ride a bicycle.

Parents who severely restrict their child's freedom of movement may suppress his tendencies to explore and to investigate, and thus inhibit the development of motivations for autonomy and independence. Some mothers find it difficult to deal with active, running, jumping, climbing children who seem to be into everything; hence, they discourage the child's exploration and his attempts to experiment. Other mothers are overprotective, tending to baby their children, discouraging independence and attempting to keep them close and clinging—perhaps because they regard independence as a threat to their own domination, control, and possession of the children. Many overprotected children become submissive and compliant; unable or afraid to make spontaneous responses; inhibited in investigating, exploring, and experimenting; shy and withdrawn in social situations. These children lack persistence; they give up readily when faced with difficult tasks or problems, probably as a result of lack of rewards for early problem-solving efforts and of their parents' tendency to solve problems for them. Since persistence is often necessary for learning academic subjects, an overprotected child may be at a disadvantage when he goes to school.

On the other hand, parental stimulation and encouragement of the child's independent achievements, exploration, and attempts at mastery may affect his later behavior in positive ways. For example, among nursery school children, those with mothers who encourage early independence and achievement tend to be more interested than others, participating in challenging and creative activities such as painting, making clay models, and reading books. When they reach school age, they are, according to personality tests, more highly motivated for achievement, and their grades are better than those of children who were not rewarded for early strivings for independence. Apparently, strong motivation to learn and to perform well in school is fostered by parental encouragement of competence and exploration early in life. Moreover, motivation for achievement appears to be a stable aspect of personality. If it develops early, it is likely to be maintained over a long span of years.

The Effects of Different Types of Home Atmosphere

The early mother-child relationships that are most important in molding a child's personality and adjustment are centered about specific needs and activities—for instance, feeding, toilet-training, curiosity, and exploration. Later on, broad, general features of the home environment and parental attitudes—rather than specific child-rearing techniques—assume greater importance and exert more influence.

The impacts of various types of home atmosphere on the personality characteristics and behavior of preschool children have been studied systematically, and longitudinally, at the Fels Institute in Yellow Springs, Ohio. To evaluate the home atmosphere in which each subject lived, a "home visitor," a highly trained and perceptive woman, visited each home and observed the interactions among the family members. On the basis of her observations, she rated each home on 30 carefully defined qualities that provide an objective, well-rounded description of its atmosphere. Examples of these qualities are warmth, possessiveness, democracy, intellectuality, restrictiveness, severity, interference, adjustment, and activity of the home. The children's personality characteristics were rated independently from systematic observations of their behavior in nursery school.

Children from "democratic" homes—which are characterized by general permissiveness, frequent conversations between parents and child, consultations about decisions—got high ratings in leadership, activity, outgoingness, assertiveness, and playfulness. Most democratic homes were also judged to be high in *warmth,* and they provided strong emotional support for a child. Children from these warm, democratic homes showed more creativity, originality, constructiveness, and curiosity than others, and they were more noncomforming and disobedient. In brief, they were highly energetic, socially active children, relatively uninhibited in expressing feelings and emotions, including protests against authorities such as teachers.

By contrast, children brought up in "controlled" homes—homes with many clearcut rules, prohibitions, and restrictions—tended to be quiet, well-behaved, shy, socially unassertive, inhibited, highly conforming, and lacking in curiosity and creativity. Those from highly "indulgent" homes, where they were babied and protected, also displayed these characteristics and, in addition, had poor motor development and strong fears of physical activity.

We can interpret these findings in terms of social learning and generalization. Permissive, democratic homes encourage and reward curiosity, exploration, experimentation, attempts to cope with new problems, and the expression of ideas and feelings. Apparently, these activities—learned and strengthened at home—generalize to the nursery school. Analogously, the child who is highly controlled or overprotected by his parents does not learn these kinds of responses, because he is discouraged from acting independently, exploring, and experimenting. He acquires timid, awkward, apprehensive, and generally conforming responses, and these become generalized from the home to the nursery school.

Maladaptive Behavior. Clinical studies show that home atmosphere is also related to general emotional adjustment. Children between the ages of four and six from democratic homes are more stable, less argumentative, more sensitive to praise and blame, more socially successful, and more considerate than children from authoritarian homes. Overattention or overindulgence at home also leads to many kinds of maladaptive, infantile behavior—for instance, crying easily, dawdling, lack of independence and persistence, withdrawal, and high dependence on adults.

Negligent mothers, who fail to supply adequate nurturance, rear children who are emotionally tense and insecure and exhibit strong attention-getting mechanisms—they show off a great deal and have many temper tantrums and aggressive outbursts. Children from calm and happy homes appear to be more secure emotionally—they are less negativistic, less jealous, less fearful, less nervous, less sulky, and less demanding of attention.

Friction between parents is probably the most common antecedent of emotional maladjustment in children. Parental tensions involving sex difficulties, lack of consideration or of cooperation, extramarital relations, poor health, conflicts about friends or relatives—any of these may inhibit the establishment of relaxed, happy parent-child relationships. And the absence of such relationships makes it difficult for the child to learn emotionally mature, adaptive responses.

Identification

Many of a child's overt responses, characteristics, attitudes, emotional reactions, and motives are acquired as a result of social learning and reward in the family and these tend to generalize to situations outside the home. Other characteristics and responses, however, appear to be acquired *without direct or immediate teaching or reward,* through *identification* with others. Identification may be regarded as a *learned drive or motive to be like another individual.* When a child identifies with someone else, he thinks, behaves, and feels as though the other person's characteristics were his own. The child is identifying with a parent when he "attempts to duplicate in his own life the ideals, attitudes, and behavior of [that] parent." The person or group with whom the child identifies is referred to as the *model* or *identificand.*

Identification is a fundamental mechanism of personality development and socialization. By identifying with his parents, a child acquires many of their characteristics and important ways of behaving, thinking, and feeling. "The boy who uses his father's words and inflections, or swaggers across the yard wearing his father's hat, is reacting to these characteristics and objects as if they were his. But in so doing he is also duplicating his father's reactions and learning to act as his father acts. In more significant aspects of behavior it is the same." * Through this kind of identification, the child acquires the family pattern of behavior. Furthermore, since his parents are generally representatives, thus carriers, of their culture, the child's identification with them provides him with attitudes, motives, ideals, values, taboos, and morals appropriate for his cultural group, social class, and role in society. The psy-

* Cameron, N., and Magaret, A. *Behavior pathology*. Boston: Houghton Mifflin, 1951, p. 61.

choanalytic term *superego* refers to the organization of ideals, attitudes, standards, and values acquired in the process of identification. Once a child has adopted his parents', and thus the culture's, moral standards, valuations and judgments, he punishes himself—largely by feeling guilty or anxious—whenever he does, or is tempted to do, something that is, in his opinion, prohibited or immoral. In addition, identification with the parent of his own sex leads to the child's *appropriate sex-typing*—the adoption of personality traits, social and emotional behavior, and attitudes considered appropriate to his own sex. "Sex-role identification has occurred when masculine or feminine behavior is no longer deliberate or imitative but automatic and generalized to all areas of the self, from style of walking and thinking to the style of sexual behavior." * Certainly direct rewards for sex-appropriate responses and social pressures for conformity play a major part in establishing sex-typing, but a child's identification with the parent of the same sex also contributes heavily.

Identification begins early in life, and is a prolonged—perhaps life-long—process. As a child matures, he continues to identify with his parents, acquiring more of their characteristics. As his social world expands, however, he finds other identification models among his peers, teachers, ministers, and heroes from fiction, movies, and TV, and he emulates their behavior, characteristics, and ideals. Thus, although a child's initial identifications are with his parents, he does not develop personality characteristics and value systems that are carbon copies of theirs. Identifications with others may result in modifications of the original parental patterns and new, different, sometimes unique models of thought and behavior may emerge.

> Thus his personality, in the end, will be built upon the basis of a long series of identifications; in some respects he will be like his parents, in some respects like each of several admired or respected teachers, in some respects like the different heroes he has encountered in fiction, biographies, the movies, etc.; in some respects like ministers, doctors, or other respected people in his community, etc. Since his personality has been derived from so many different sources, it will be a complex and unique organization.†

Research on Identification

Identification may be at least partially an unconscious process. There are a number of theories about the motives underlying the child's identification with his parents. According to one theory, which is related to psychoanalysis, the preschool child, observing his parents' status, powers, privileges, pleasures, and mastery of the environment, becomes envious of them. But he cannot express his envy, or anger or hostility connected with this envy, because being highly dependent on his parents, he cannot risk losing their love and attention. Consequently, he begins to identify with them, adopting their behavior and char-

* McCandless, B. R. *Children and adolescents,* p. 330.
† Sappenfield, B. R. *Personality dynamics.* New York: Knopf, 1954, p. 297.

acteristics, as though he believed that if he were similar to them, he would possess their envied attributes.

Another, quite different, theory of the motives underlying identification is based on the principles of learning. This theory maintains that the parent who loves the child and gratifies his needs becomes associated with feelings of pleasure and comfort; the parent's behavior and characteristics are also associated with these positive feelings, or in learning theory terms, they acquire reward value for the child. By adopting and imitating his parents' behavior and characteristics, the child experiences the feelings of gratification originally associated with his parents; in a sense, he supplies his own rewards.

The findings of a number of empirical studies support this second theory by showing that warm, gratifying parent-child relationships foster the establishment of strong identifications with the parents. One study demonstrated that sons of warm, permissive, easygoing fathers frequently play the father's role—an indication of their identification with the father—in a projective doll play situation, whereas boys whose fathers lack these characteristics seldom play this role.

In another study, a large group of adolescent boys and their fathers responded to identical questionnaires on personality. Boys whose responses to the questionnaire were highly similar to their fathers' were assumed to be closely identified with their fathers; boys whose responses differed widely from their fathers' were considered low in father-identification. The boys were then given a projective test—finishing incomplete stories—which revealed their attitudes toward their parents. Boys with high father-identification regarded their fathers as warmer and more rewarding than the other boys regarded theirs, suggesting that the basis of identification is love and respect for the identificand.

Experimental Studies of Imitation. The results of two ingenious experiments on the imitation of models tend to confirm these findings on the relationship between the rewarding qualities of the parent and the child's identification with him. In one of these experiments, one group of nursery school boys and girls—the *nurtured*, or *rewarded*, group—had two periods of interaction with a young woman who was to serve as a model. She gave a child toys and sat near him in the experimental room while he played, responding to his bids for help and attention, and in other ways maintaining consistently warm and rewarding interactions. A matched group of nursery school children, the *nonnurtured* group, also played with toys in the experimental room but the experimenter busied herself in a far corner of the room and had no interactions with any child.

The test of imitation was conducted immediately after the second social interaction session. The model and the child played a game (actually, a discrimination learning problem), guessing which of two boxes contained a prize. The model always took the first turn, showing the child the correct choice. In addition, however, she exhibited certain verbal and motor behaviors that were totally irrelevant to obtaining the reward. For example, when beginning the trial she remarked "Here I go" and then marched slowly but deliberately toward the two boxes, repeating "March, march, march."

The research was of course designed to determine whether the nurtured group would be more imitative of the model than the nonnurtured group. The results demonstrated clearly that this was the case. Those who experienced rewarding interactions with the model imitated her marching and her remarks to a significantly greater extent than the subjects who had cold and distant relationships with her. Assuming that this kind of imitation is analogous to imitation based on identification, we can conlude that, as in the studies reported above, nurturant, warm, and rewarding relationships with a model—an experimenter or a parent—foster the child's identification with that model.

Another, more complex experiment made use of three-person groups consisting of a nursery school child and two adult models, to some extent reproducing a family situation. In the first interaction of the three, one of the adults was a dispenser of desirable toys, games, and cookies; in brief, he controlled rewards and gratifications. Since the child was informed the supply of these things was limited, he viewed the other adult as a rival, competing for things he wanted.

Following this social interaction, the subjects participated in the same discrimination learning task, guessing which box contained the prize, used in the experiment reported above. Both models showed the child a correct solution and he was then given an opportunity to imitate them. Before beginning his trial, however, each model selected his own "thinking cap" from an array of available hats and put it on in his own special way. He then assumed certain distinctive postures, and repeated certain phrases. While performing the task—that is, while going to the boxes to make his choice—each model exhibited many novel, distinctive motor and verbal responses, all of them irrelevant to the discrimination task. All this was done in the presence of the child. The child's imitation score was the number of his postural, motor, and verbal responses that matched the model's.

Children imitated the model who possessed rewarding power significantly more frequently than they imitated the rival. These data fail to support the theory that identification is a consequence of a rivalrous, envious interaction between the child and the model. Children clearly identify with the source of rewarding power rather than with the competitor for these rewards.

Sex-Typing. Since sex-typing, the adoption of behavior appropriate to one's own sex, is one of the major consequences of identification with the like-sexed parent, measures of sex-typing can be used as indications of degree of identification with this parent. Thus, among the adolescent boys in the identification study mentioned above, the boys who identified highly with their fathers were more masculine in interests and attitudes (according to a masculinity test) than those who were low in father-identification.

Degree of sex-typing can also be evaluated by tests indicating whether a child's interests, and his preferences for toys, clothes, and games are typically those of his own or the opposite sex. In one study, five- and six-year-old boys and girls were given such tests and classified as high or low in appropriate sex-typing. Subsequently, they participated in a doll play "game" in which they played out, and completed, nine simple stories involving a mother, father, a child doll (of the child's own sex), and simple furniture. The following is an example of a test story:

> The child is having fun playing with some toys. Mommy and daddy say, "It's time to go to bed now." The child says, "I don't want to go to bed now." Then the child throws a toy on the floor and it breaks. What happens?

Each child's perceptions of his own parents—as nurturant, tender, warm, and helpful, or as punitive and frustrating—were determined from his responses to these stories. (In interpreting a child's doll play, it is assumed that the child's description of the mother and father dolls reflect his perceptions of his own parents.) The mothers of the subjects were also interviewed about their relationships with their children.

Compared with boys low in masculinity, highly masculine boys perceived their fathers as significantly more nurturant and rewarding. Analogously, highly feminine girls described their mothers as warmer and more gratifying than the other girls did. The data from maternal interviews, corroborating the doll play findings, showed that the fathers of the highly masculine boys were warmer and more affectionate than the other boys' fathers. Moreover, they were more interested in their sons, and spent more time with them. The mothers of the highly feminine girls also had warmer relationships with their daughters and were more interested in them than the mothers of the other, less strongly sex-typed, girls.

Aggressiveness, generally regarded as a masculine characteristic in our culture, is also acquired, at least in part, through identification. In one experiment, a group of nursery school children were shown adult models expressing aggression and afterward were subjected to a mild degree of frustration. Another group of children were exposed only to nonaggressive models, and a control group had no exposure to any models. Both of these latter groups experienced the same degree of frustration as the first group. Following the frustrating experience, each child was taken to another room where his behavior could be observed.

Those who had been exposed to aggressive models made substantially more aggressive responses than the children of the other two groups. Much of the behavior of the first group was clearly imitative of the models' physical and verbal aggression. Since aggression is sex-typed, it is not surprising that the modeling influence was most pronounced for boys who had been exposed to a male aggressive model.

In another study, kindergarten boys who were highly identified with aggressive fathers—fathers who punished them—exhibited frequent and intense aggression in doll play. Girls who were strongly identified with highly aggressive mothers—mothers who used physical punishment frequently—were also highly aggressive in doll play, whereas girls who were identified with mothers who seldom punished them tended to be mild and nonaggressive. In short, identification with a like-sexed parent leads to a resemblance in degree of aggressiveness.

Development of Conscience. The development of a strong conscience, another consequence of identification, also appears to be based on satisfactory parent-child relationships. The results of one study show that maternal warmth is positively correlated with strength of conscience, and boys with accepting fathers are more likely to develop strong consciences than boys who are rejected by their fathers.

A high degree of conscience is promoted by the use of love-oriented disciplinary techniques, that is, techniques in which love is given or withheld to reward or to punish the child. Praise and reasoning as disciplinary techniques are associated with high conscience in children, whereas physical punishment is related to poor conscience development. The use of love-oriented disciplinary techniques is only effective for warm and loving mothers who maintain strong and affectionate relationships with their children. Children are in fact most likely to develop a high level of conscience if they have affectionate mothers who threaten to withdraw love as punishment for disobedience. Conscience appears to be a consequence of an identification based on the child's fear of loss of love of an otherwise warm and loving parent.

> . . . Withdrawing love where little exists is meaningless. If the mother is relatively cold to begin with, then using withdrawal of love should have little effect on conscience development. The pattern most calculated to produce "high conscience" should be that of mothers who are usually warm and loving and then, as a method of control, threaten this affectionate relationship.
>
> . . . this is indeed the case. The children most prone to behave in the ways we have considered indicative of having a well-developed conscience were those whose mothers were relatively warm toward them but who made their love contingent on the child's good behavior. These were the children who truly were risking the loss of love when they misbehaved.*

Failure in Identification

The child who does not have warm and affectionate relationships with his parents may fail to establish strong identification with them. Consequently, he may not acquire certain characteristics, motives, attitudes, and ideals essential to his adjustment and happiness in his culture, and to his social and emotional security. For example, a boy's failure to identify with his father or with other men may lead to effeminate behavior and attitudes. Total failure to identify with

* Sears, R. R., Maccoby, E. E., and Levin, H. *Patterns of child rearing*. New York: Harper & Row, 1957, pp. 388–389.

members of his own sex may result in homosexuality. Many cases of juvenile delinquency may also be interpreted as a lack of identification with the family's moral and ethical standards of behavior.

Modifications of Family Influences

Although this chapter has stressed familial influences in personality development, don't underestimate the impacts of other social groups and agencies on a child. Unfortunately, there have been few systematic studies of the influences of peers, neighborhood, school, church, and mass media (newspapers, movies, television, and so on) on a child's personality development. Nevertheless, it is obvious that in the course of making new social contacts, reading, and viewing movies and television, the child finds new identificands among peers, neighbors, teachers, clergy, and heroes of fiction, movies, and TV. By emulating the behavior of these models, behavior patterns acquired at home may be modified or new responses may be established. In some cases, the new identifications reinforce and strengthen responses learned in the family setting; in other cases, the new behavior may be different—or even opposite—from what is learned at home.

Some of the values and goals sanctioned in the broader community may be different from those of a child's parents and the discrepancy may produce conflict for him. For example, a middle-class child learns to control his aggressive feelings and to inhibit overt aggression. If his playmates are also middle-class children, this learning will be reinforced in the neighborhood. But if he lives in a lower-class neighborhood and goes to a lower-class school, his peers may expect him to act aggressively when he is angry and will reward him for such behavior. When family and peer group expectancies are at variance, as in this case, a child may be in conflict about which set of standards to adopt. If his identification with his parents is strong, he is not likely to adopt values contrary to theirs; if his identifications are weak, or if the peer group pressures are great (as they are likely to be in adolescence; see page 92), he is more likely to adopt the peers' values.

SITUATIONAL DETERMINANTS OF BEHAVIOR

The data reviewed in the last two chapters make it clear that the child's basic personality structure—the organization of his established traits—is determined, to some extent, by his biological makeup, to a greater extent by his cultural group membership, and, most importantly, by his intimate relationships with others, particularly with members of his family. But a child's behavior, and the personality characteristics manifested at any particular time are functions of *both personality and an immediately present situation.*

To illustrate, let us look at extreme behavior in a crisis. A child may customarily be secure, relaxed, and calm, his everyday behavior in school reflecting these characteristics. But faced with an event such as fire, storm, or injury, he may display strong fear or panic. Children who are ordinarily anxious, fearful, and excitable may react with even greater fears and more panic in such situations. To cite a less extreme example, a youngster may be anxious and aggressive when he is with his tense, highly punitive parents, but he may behave much more calmly when he is with a relaxed, friendly nursery school teacher.

Frustration and Aggression

Everyone occasionally encounters a frustration—an obstacle interfering with the achievement of a desired goal. From a research point of view frustration is a *situational* variable; reactions to it have been studied extensively, both experimentally and in natural settings. One of the most common reactions is aggression. In nursery school, for example, aggressive conflicts between children increase when the amount of play space is limited and when, consequently, there are more frustrations and interferences.

Children subjected to experimentally produced frustrations are likely to react with aggressive responses, especially if they are in a permissive situation where aggression is not likely to bring punishment. In one study, preschool boys and girls were observed playing with dolls for two 30-minute sessions. During the first, they were allowed to play freely. But before the second session, one group of subjects, the *failure,* or *frustration, group,* worked at extremely difficult tasks that made them feel unsuccessful and frustrated. The *control* group was not experimentally frustrated before the second doll play session.

In the second session, both groups displayed more aggression than they had during the first play period, probably because the permissive atmosphere permitted such expression. The frustration group, however, showed significantly *greater increases in aggression* than the control group. Apparently, the experience of frustration elicited the subsequent heightened aggressiveness.

Of course, the degree of frustration is not the only determinant of the intensity or amount of aggressive reactions. Of children experiencing the same frustration, some become violently aggressive while others become only mildly so. Why? Because from past experiences, some children acquire high degrees of "tolerance for frustration" (marked ability to endure frustration without becoming upset). Preschool children who, according to tests, have developed such tolerance display significantly less aggression than children in the same nursery school who experience the same frustrations but have lower tolerances.

Moreover, children differ in the intensity of their acquired fears of punishment for aggressiveness. Among the boys studied at one juvenile institution, those with strong fears of punishment for such behavior were less aggressive than their peers who were relatively unafraid, even though the two groups were in the same situation (institution) and experienced the same frustrations. Apparently, then, the intensity of a child's aggression is a function not only of the situation—although that is important—but also of the personality structure he has developed.

Frustration and Regression

Aggression is only one of many possible reactions to frustration. Under some circumstances, some children *regress* after frustration, that is, they exhibit already "outgrown" immature responses. For example, if a three-year-old child has given up his bottle in favor of drinking from a cup, but begins to demand a bottle again when he sees his young brother with one, he is exhibiting *regression*.

A well-known experiment by Roger Barker, Tamara Dembo, and Kurt Lewin showed that regression may be a reaction to frustration. They observed nursery school children, individually, for a half hour of free play with a standard set of play materials, fully recording the playtime behavior and rating it for maturity and constructiveness.

Later, each subject was brought into an experimental room where he found the same standard play materials, but now these were presented together with a very attractive set of new toys. In this situation, the child soon became absorbed in play with the new toys, neglecting the standard set. While he was so absorbed, an experimenter quietly and unobtrusively collected the less attractive, standard set of toys and moved them to another part of the room. He then led the child to that part of the room and lowered a wire screen, thus making the more attractive toys inaccessible, though still visible. In this frustrating situation—seeing the more attractive toys, but being unable to play with them—the child again played with the standard toys he had played with originally. The experimenter could again rate the maturity and constructiveness of play.

The children's play regressed considerably, on the average, when they were frustrated. It was less mature, less constructive, and less creative than it had been in the original free-play (nonfrustrating) situation with the same toys. In short, frustration produced *regression,* a reduction in the level of maturity.

Many children reacted to the frustration by trying to escape or withdraw, or by behaving aggressively. They approached the inaccessible part of the room, pleaded with the experimenter to be allowed out, or hit or kicked the screen or the experimenter. Those who withdrew most or became most aggressive also regressed most in their play activities.

Another, more recent study using the same technique demonstrated that the tendency to regress or behave aggressively following this frustration depends on a subject's previous experiences, frustration tolerance, and ability to control immature, impulsive reactions—as well as on the situation (which was the same for all subjects). Children with high frustration tolerance, as measured by tests, regressed less in play and were less aggressive when denied access to the more attractive toys. In summary, frustration tends to arouse aggression or regression but the intensity of these reactions varies with a child's personality structure and earlier learning.

Situational Determinants of Dependency

In general, a child's dependency is determined by his developmental history, but manifestations of dependency may be strongly affected by the immediate situation. This was demonstrated in one experimental study in which preschool children played alone for 20 minutes, and were thus deprived of social stimulation, before participating in a simple learning experiment. A control group of children did not experience this kind of deprivation, but were presented with the same learning problem. The reward for correct responses during learning was verbal approval by the experimenter.

The experimental, deprived subjects were more responsive to this reward; that is, they learned faster than the control group did. Apparently, absence of social interaction—and the concomitant lack of gratification of dependency needs—leads to a greater need for attention and approval (dependence on others) that increases the reward value of verbal expressions of approval. Furthermore, children who are characteristically more dependent, according to observation of their behavior in nursery school, reacted most favorably to adult approval in the experimental situation. In this age group, approval by a woman experimenter was more effective for boys, whereas approval by a male experimenter was more effective for girls.

Another experimental study demonstrates even more clearly that deprivation of social contact and reassurance heightens a child's dependency. A female experimenter, while watching a group of nursery school children playing freely with toys, gave them a great deal of attention and affection, thus gratifying their dependency needs. Then, abruptly, she stopped talking to them, withdrawing her attention and nurturance, and refusing to answer their questions. In psychological terms, after gratifying the children's dependency needs for a period of time, she frustrated them. A control group of children received consistent dependency-need gratification; that is, the experimenter did not withdraw her affection and attention or frustrate their dependency needs. Later, while learning something, the children in the frustrated group appeared to be much more highly motivated to seek praise by the experimenter—that is, to be nurtured and to have their dependency needs gratified—than the control group. Apparently, gratification of dependency needs followed by frustration (withdrawal of gratification) heightened these needs. This was particularly true for the girls.

As in the study reported above, boys who were ordinarily highly dependent reacted most strongly to this frustration; they became highly motivated to receive praise from the experimenter. Independent boys, however, were not so much affected by withdrawal of nurturance and attention. We may conclude that although deprivation of nurturance and warmth is likely to strengthen a young child's dependency needs, at least temporarily, the intensity of his reactions will be conditioned by his personality structure and earlier experiences.

The Behavior of Peers. A young child's behavior is likely to be swayed by his playmates' reactions. For example, when playing with companions who use force, threats, and shame to attain goals, kindergarten children—even those who are ordinarily mild-mannered—tend to act more dominantly. When they are with playmates who are socially more mature and constructive, children are likely to become more cooperative, to seek common purposes in activity, and to use requests and suggestions rather than force in social interactions. Although these findings refer to the *immediate* effects of a playmate's behavior, viewed as a situational variable, frequent and prolonged interactions with a dominant or cooperative playmate—especially a loved and admired one—may lead a child to adopt one or the other of these characteristics.

Practical Implications. These studies of reactions to frustration indicate that parents and teachers may expect aggressive outbursts or regressions to immature behavior—such as thumbsucking, or bedwetting—when a child is under stress or feels frustrated—for example, when there are tensions in the family or when a new sibling arrives. When deprived of gratification of dependency needs—when, for example, his mother is less nurturant than usual—the child may be expected to behave in more dependent ways. When a child regresses, acts aggressively, or in an unusually dependent manner, his mother may be alerted that the child is frustrated, and she can look for the source of the frustration and try to remove or alleviate it. If she is successful, the child's immaturity or aggressiveness will diminish and he will behave more maturely and constructively.

Punishment may not be effective in reducing or eliminating a child's aggressive behavior. In fact, punishment may act as a frustration and may sometimes lead to an increased incidence of aggression toward others, although it may reduce the child's overt aggression toward the punisher. Analogously, punishment for dependency, like deprivation of affection and attention in the experiments cited above, may lead to an increase in dependency need and dependent behavior.

The Modification of Children's Personalities

That situations can lead to changes in young children's behavior demonstrates that, at this age, personality characteristics are not fixed or immutable. As his world expands, a child encounters many new situations and has many new social interactions that may produce radical alterations in personality structure and behavior.

Experiences on the playground or in school may promote self-confidence in a child who was previously grossly lacking in this characteristic. A shy, sullen, and withdrawn child, the product of an unsatisfactory, harsh, and restrictive home environment, may expand in a permissive nursery school with warm, understanding teachers, becoming lively, happy, and creative. Similarly, a boy who is unable to identify with a cold, unkind father, may be retarded in the acquisition of sex-typed characteristics and interests. If he forms a strong friendship with a highly masculine boy, identification may then promote, and accelerate, the boy's sex-typing, compensating, at least in part, for earlier difficulties in this area.

On the other hand, unfortunate school or neighborhood experiences may undermine the beneficial effects of good parent-child relationships. For example, if his parents have been warm, gentle, and permissive, a child may enter school feeling secure, self-possessed, and confident. But if he is below average in intelligence, or lacking in motivation to study, he may experience crushing failures in school, and, as a consequence, become frustrated and aggressive. He may change from a socially outgoing and pleasant youngster into an unhappy, withdrawn, socially maladjusted one. In short, encountering new situations—particularly social relationships—may lead to major readjustments and significant alterations in a child's personality and behavior.

Research Evidence. Even simple social learning may lead to important changes in personality characteristics. For example, in one relevant experiment, 12 nursery school children with immature reactions to failure (retreating, giving up easily, crying, sulking) were given special training designed to increase their perseverance and independence in solving difficult problems. A control group of 12 children who were only slightly immature received no special training. In the training, the experimenter met with each child a number of times, introducing him to problems and encouraging him to work them out independently. As training progressed, the problems became more complex and difficult, but the youngsters became more interested and gained continuously in independence. They requested less help and persevered longer in their attempts to solve the problems. Spontaneous comments showing self-confidence (for instance, "It's a hard problem but I'm getting better all the time") became more frequent.

After training, the control and experimental groups were given new difficult puzzles to solve. The trained group showed significantly more increase in independence than the controls, more interest than they had shown originally, and they worked harder than they did before training. Crying, sulking, aggressive outbursts, and destruction occurred infrequently as reactions to difficult problems. Mature, independent responses, learned during the training, were apparently generalized to the new problems. As for the control group, however, in the second test, they did not show significant improvements in their attempts to solve difficult problems or in their reactions to frustration.

From this and similar experiments, we may conclude that young children's immature and maladaptive responses to frustration can be improved easily. With relatively little training—and fairly simple training at that—a child may acquire greater frustration tolerance and increased independence, persistence, and a calm approach that may generalize to other potentially frustrating situations.

6 The Development of Social Behavior

The preceding chapters on personality development necessarily included some discussion of important aspects of social behavior, for any evaluation of personality is based largely on observations of social behavior—that is, a child's interactions with others, especially with peers. For example, we judge children to be highly aggressive if they attack, or quarrel with, peers frequently; domineering if they try to control or boss others; and dependent if they seek a great deal of aid or reassurance in social interactions. General attitudes toward parents and toward the world at large are strongly influenced, as we have seen, by early parent-child relationships. In a sense, then, our present discussion of the development of social behavior and the antecedents of individual differences in such behavior began in earlier sections dealing with personality characteristics and attitudes.

Our interests in the present chapter are the growth and development of some other social characteristics; the structure of social groups and friendship patterns in childhood; and opinions and attitudes toward others (peers, parents, minority groups); and finally socially unacceptable behavior, specifically, juvenile delinquency.

Psychologists can study children's social behavior and development by means of careful, naturalistic observation or experimental methods. In *observation,* an investigator usually finds a good look-out station in a nursery school, playground, or social club and, usually using a time-sampling method, systematically records the children's interactions. For example, if he were interested in *aggressive behavior,* he would note all instances of hitting others, destroying toys, and shouting at the teacher or other children. Or he could use a checklist with many items of aggression listed and check the appropriate ones as various behaviors occurred. In *experiments* on the development of social behavior, he would place children in a specially devised situation, and observe and record their reactions to the situation and to other children. Let us look at some examples of research on this subject.

SOCIAL BEHAVIOR AT VARIOUS AGE LEVELS

Social Behavior during the Preschool Years

In one cross-sectional study, the interactions between pairs of babies of the same age, placed together in a playpen with standard toys, were observed for a four-minute period. With increased age between six and 25 months, interactions progressed steadily from initial indifference toward the partner to social interest and cooperative play. Infants between six and eight months of age generally ignored each other, each treating the other as he did the toys. There were, though, a few social contacts, which were limited to looking, smiling, and grasping the partner. Babies between nine and 13 months of age gave some attention to their partners and fights occurred if one child attempted to snatch a toy from the other. Between 14 and 18 months, attention to the partner as an individual increased considerably, and, simultaneously, conflicts over toys decreased. In the last age period studied, between 19 and 25 months, there were more social contacts such as looking and smiling at the partner, and play became far more personal, cooperative, and friendly.

Social development is markedly accelerated during the nursery school period when a child's contacts with peers become more frequent and intense. In one well-known study, time samples of interactions in nursery school were categorized according to a hierarchy of increasingly mature and cooperative social responses. There were six categories and scores: unoccupied behavior (—3); solitary play (independent of other children; —2); onlooker behavior (watching, but not playing with, others; —1); parallel play (playing alongside, but not with, others; +1); associative play (playing with others in joint projects, sharing materials; +2); cooperative, or organized, play (each child making his own contribution to joint play; +3).

The study showed that as preschool children grow older, they spend less time in relatively nonsocial activities (those low in the scale), and more advanced types of social behavior become increasingly frequent. The most rudimentary form of social interaction, parallel play, is characteristic of two-year-olds, but relatively uncommon among children four and five years of age, who indulge in more associative or cooperative play.

Undoubtedly, many factors account for these modifications in social behavior. With greater maturity, a child's greater physical and intellectual abilities enable him to participate in more complex, cooperative activities. Moreover, older children have been rewarded more frequently for outgoing and friendly responses, and at nursery school and on playgrounds, cooperative, socially oriented responses bring further satisfactions; hence, these responses become stronger and are more apt to be repeated. At the same time, spending time without activity and merely observing are discouraged by parents and nursery school teachers, so they become weaker responses and tend to drop away.

Preschool Friendships. The number of social conflicts and quarrels decreases, and friendly contacts between children become more pronounced between the ages of two and five. During these years, children form their first friendships, generally, but not exclusively, with others of their own sex. Friendship patterns change markedly with age. Between the ages of two and three, the *number* of friends increases; after this age, the primary change is in the *closeness of attachment* to a few particular children.

A socially oriented and responsive preschool child seeks out companions and has a variety of contacts with them. In the course of learning the modes of social interaction, such a child has both satisfying and frustrating experiences, and, consequently, exhibits social responses that seem to be contradictory. For example, preschool friends tend to argue more frequently with each other than children who rarely associate with one another. Highly aggressive nursery school children are also most sympathetic with their classmates, responding most readily to their distress. The child who grabs a toy from a playmate at one moment may rush to comfort a crying, unhappy child the next.

Popular children and leaders can be distinguished as early as the nursery school period. Some children are continually being sought out as playmates; others are consistently shunned and avoided by their nursery school classmates. Some youngsters ordinarily assume a dominant role in their relationships with peers, while others are usually passive followers. Moreover, leadership styles are clearly discernible: diplomats control others subtly, by indirect suggestion, whereas bullies boss and force others to comply with their wishes.

Social Conflicts. There are great individual differences in proneness to conflicts, but the average nursery school child between two and four years of age is involved in some sort of conflict every five minutes. Boys tend to participate in more conflicts and make more attacks, whereas girls tend to argue more. These sex differences are more pronounced among older nursery school children, reflecting their more firmly established sex-typing of behavior.

In general, the interactions of preschool youngsters are more characteristically cooperative and friendly than unfriendly, hostile, or competitive. Even the most highly aggressive preschool children actually make more friendly than aggressive responses. Aggressiveness, incidentally, tends to be a fairly stable characteristic, the frequency of a child's conflicts during nursery school being a reliable indicator of his proneness to conflict in kindergarten.

Competition. Competitiveness appears as early as the ages of three or four, according to the findings of one study in which pairs of children were given a pile of blocks and each one was instructed to compete, to build something prettier or bigger than his companions. Those between the ages of four and six compete with considerable intensity, grabbing materials from each other, disregarding the other child's feelings and intentions, and refusing to give help or materials. By this age, competitive motives are strong enough to produce improvement in performance when a child is competing with someone else. As children advance in age, they become acutely aware of the culture's prevalent attitudes toward, and consistent rewards for, competition; hence, they adopt competitive values and motivations.

Boys compete more than girls and lower-middle-class children are more competitive than those from the upper middle class. Highly competitive children often come from democratic, freedom-giving homes, but they are likely to have histories of conflicts with siblings. During the preschool period, competition and aggression appear to be relatively independent; that is, the most competitive children are not ordinarily the most aggressive. Among older children and adults, these motives are likely to be more closely associated.

Friendships in Middle Childhood

Social relationships of the school years are more extensive, more intense, and more influential than those of the earlier years. The major social developments of this period reflect children's increased socialization, their more firmly established sex-typing, and the stronger social pressures for conformity to group standards.

Preschool friendships, being casual, unstable, and transient, probably have relatively few important or enduring effects on a child's personality. In middle childhood, the situation is different. With the exception of his parents and teachers, the child's close friends are probably his most important "socializers," and they have direct and powerful impacts on his personality and social development.

From roughly ages seven to 12, youngsters are strongly concerned with their gang, an informal group with a fairly rapid turnover in membership. Later on, between the ages of 10 and 14, highly structured groups—groups with formal organization and membership requirements, such as Boy Scouts and Girl Scouts—assume greater importance, especially among middle-class children.

The social relationships of these years may have far-reaching influences. The child's choice of extracurricular games, reading, movies, radio and television programs, are undoubtedly swayed by his peers' opinions and suggestions. These media, in turn, may provide new identification models and new evaluations of certain types of values, attitudes, characteristics, and behavior.

In choosing friends, elementary school children, particularly in the sixth, seventh, and eighth grades, prefer members of their own sex. Most boys between the ages of six and eight, however, ignore sex in play groupings, choosing girls on their sides in games as freely as they choose boys. At the age of eight, approximately, attitudes seem to change and associations with members of the opposite sex decrease sharply. By 11 or 12, boys and girls are almost completely segregated from each other in play groups and in social gatherings. "This stage of segregation began with haughty aloofness, became apparent contempt, and active hostility, and then changed to shy withdrawal which seemed to mark the end of this period and the beginning of adolescent heterosexuality after puberty." *

The segregation of the sexes during these years is probably related to the process of sex-typing and to the intense cultural pressures on children to adopt sex-appropriate behavior. Peer groups facilitate the development of sex identification and sex-typing by rewarding the boys' "real boy" and the girls' "real girl" activities, and punishing "sissy" behavior in boys and, to a lesser extent, "tomboyishness" in girls. By the age of nine, many activities, interests, and attitudes are clearly sex-typed, and there are striking sex differences in play, reading, movie, and television preferences and in vocational choices. Boys between the ages of eight and eleven are principally interested in playing active, vigorous, competitive games involving muscular skills and dexterity, whereas girls of this age engage in more quiet, sedentary activities. The reading interests of the two sexes are similar until the age of eight or nine, but, afterward, boys prefer adventure, exploration, travel, biography, mystery, and science stories and girls choose fairy tales, animal stories, and romances. The most popular occupational choices of boys of this age are scientist, aviator, or pilot, while girls aspire to more feminine activities such as teaching and nursing.

* Campbell, E. H. The social-sex development of children. *Genet. Psychol. Monogr.*, 1939, Vol. 21, No. 4, p. 465.

The sex-segregated peer groups of this age provide appropriate outlets for already developed sex-typed interests. Others of the same sex are more likely to have the same needs and interests, and hence to make satisfying, rewarding companions.

Of course, similarity of sex is not the only influence on friendship during the elementary school years. When asked to name their best friends, children generally choose youngsters from their own neighborhood or classroom, and those having highly esteemed personality characteristics. To illustrate, children in the second grade stress externals in choosing friends—a nice home, good looks, and having money to spend. Sixth graders, on the other hand, emphasize personal characteristics—friendliness, cheerfulness, tidiness, and cleanliness.

Studies of children's friendships provide no evidence that opposites attract. Rather, pairs of friends tend to resemble each other in social maturity, chronological age, height, weight, and general intelligence. Capable, friendly, energetic, responsive, daring children are attracted to each other, probably because they understand, and can satisfy, each other's needs. Other children are often attracted to those with these characteristics, but they are usually rejected.

Friendships of middle childhood are fairly unstable. Since interests fluctuate rapidly at this time, "old" friends may no longer provide the gratifications they provided earlier, and, consequently, friendships may be terminated and new friends substituted. With advancing age, interests become more crystallized and friendships are likely to be more stable and enduring.

The Social Patterns of Adolescents

Adolescents' social relationships are more complex, and have more ramifications, than younger children's. As has been noted, the adolescent's social situation is a particularly difficult one, since he lives simultaneously in the two worlds of children and adults, in a kind of marginal or overlapping status, not knowing where he belongs. All at once he has many new urgent, conflicting demands put on him. For example, he is expected to choose a vocation and to achieve some independence from his family. In addition, his sex drive increases as a result of hormonal changes, and he must cope with strong, forbidden impulses. Finally, since he has greater mobility, his social world broadens and he can maintain friendships over a wider geographical area. Earlier, most of his peers and friends were from his own neighborhood and social-class group, but in high school he is likely to meet boys and girls from other parts of his community and from other ethnic and cultural groups. From them, he may learn new attitudes, customs, and value systems.

Adolescent Cliques. Among his peers, the most influential—the ones with whom he identifies most strongly—are the members of his own small, select group, or *clique*. These peers, who generally come from the same socioeconomic class background, tend to be alike in personality and interests and to share common purposes and values. Cliques are based on personal compatibility, congeniality, and close ties of affection and mutual admiration. Basic orientations toward the future also play a determining role, however; those who plan to go on to college are motivated to academic achievement and become friends, whereas those who remain in school only because the law requires them to be there tend to go together. The former prefer friends who are serious-minded, talented, and enthusiastic, the latter generally want friends who are energetic, good as listeners, athletic, and appreciative of practical jokes.

Mutual interests—in writing, social activities, athletics, motorcycles—tend to bring people together. In early adolescence, shared preferences for games and sports and the ability to do exciting things together are central in friendship formation, but, in later adolescence, acceptability to members of the opposite sex (particularly among girls) becomes a more important criterion. Friendships are also related to similarities in social maturity (which, in early adolescence, is correlated with degree of physical maturity), in mental age, sociability, criticalness of self and others, extroversion, degree of conformity or rebellion, social skills, and know-how.

Functions of Peer Groups. Although he is seeking some independence from his family, an adolescent has strong needs for support while finding himself and establishing his place in society. Consequently, his dependency on peer groups increases considerably and acceptance by peers becomes surpassingly important. In line with this, adolescents in general put a higher premium on getting along with others, on being popular and friendly, than on being a good student or successful in life and work.

His peer group actually serves as a teacher for an adolescent, by helping him to learn social skills and attitudes and assisting in the adoption of adult standards. He is likely to adopt the fashions, values, beliefs, and fads of the peer group without examination, for, uncertain about how to achieve adult status, the adolescent feels reassured if he behaves as the others do. In fact, he worries if he feels that he is different from the others.

The peer group thus aids in the achievement of independence from family, not only by gratifying some of the adolescent's persisting dependency needs, but also by providing moral backing for his own demands for independence. By sticking together and behaving alike, adolescents try to protect themselves from what they perceive as the coercions, interferences, and restrictions imposed by adults.

Peer-Group Influences. In the light of the above, it is not surprising to find that the influence of intimate peers is greater at adolescence than at any previous stage, particularly with respect to moral values and character. An intensive study of moral development among adolescents in a midwestern town showed that

The peer group gives rewards and punishments to its members on account of their moral behavior. Those who are honest, responsible, loyal, kind, and self-controlled tend to be rewarded. It is not moral qualities alone, however, that determine whether a child will be rewarded or punished by his peer group. Operating in addition to the moral qualities are such non-moral qualities as diffuse geniality, and skill in games, which sometimes overshadow the moral qualities in determining the status of a child in the peer group. In general, though, the forming of stable, positive relationships within the peer group is indicative of sound character development, while inability to make friends may indicate the opposite. . . .

The peer group provides a basis for learning the major social loyalities. As the first social group which the child meets outside of his family, it tends to condition his attitude toward social groups in general. If he enjoys the peer group, he is likely to approach all groups with the expectation of liking them. Loyalty to nation, to community, and to a professional or working group probably depends upon the learning of loyalty to the smaller and more intimate groups of the family and the peer group.

The peer group helps a child build a rational foundation of moral behavior. By a rational foundation is meant a set of moral values and habits which are coherent and consistent with one another and which are subject to revision and redefinition on the basis of experience. For example, in the playing of games a child learns to respect the rules, which means that he learns the morality of the game. Then he learns to modify the rules of the game in agreement with his peers to make the game fit changing circumstances, such as the size of a playing field, the number of players, and the type of play equipment available. Thus he learns to respect rules, which is the essence of morality; but he also learns to modify rules on a rational basis. He learns a flexible, cooperative, rational morality which is essential for good citizenship in a changing democratic society.*

An adolescent peer group ordinarily reinforces and strengthens the values that members have acquired from parents, values that are approved by their social class and community. The group rewards what it regards as positive social and moral values and severely punishes antisocial or disapproved behavior. "The peer group appears to be less an originator than a reinforcer of moral values and behavior patterns developed in the family. Adolescents, as a whole, prove to admire, respect, and reward very much the same moral behavior as do the 'respectable' members of the adult community: their parents, their teachers. . . ." †

Boy-Girl Relationships during Adolescence. During the junior high school years, particularly the eighth or ninth grades, boys and girls are at distinctly different levels of maturity. The girls tend to be young ladies and are often interested in boys, but their male contemporaries are not generally interested in girls. At school dances, girls tower over, and seem to drag around, boys who would rather be playing baseball. At this age, girls have more problems concerning social life and heterosexual behavior than boys do.

All this changes around the sophomore year of high school, when boys

* Peck, R. F., and Havighurst, R. J. *The psychology of character development.* New York: Wiley, 1960, pp. 139–140.

† *Ibid.,* p. 182.

begin to catch up with girls in biological and social maturity, and in interest in the opposite sex. Boys' and girls' interests now begin to complement each other, and they pay more attention to one another. Dating, which is intimately related to prestige and status, becomes a central concern for both sexes. And problems of "getting along" with the opposite sex, arrangements for dating, and moral issues of heterosexual relationships are dominant themes in adolescent conversations. Even during the college years, about 30 per cent of bull-sessions are devoted to such topics as petting, sexual freedom, marriage, and birth control.

Young adolescents are understandably insecure and uncertain about relationships with the opposite sex, and, unfortunately, American adult culture provides relatively little guidance in these matters. Boys and girls tend to meet at some sort of hangout where they generally go with a few friends of their own sex, expecting to meet and mingle, casually and informally, with members of the opposite sex. During high school, double, or even triple, dates, are common and serve to bolster everyone's courage and security.

When asked desirable characteristics of dates, high school boys emphasize physical appearance, considerateness, and good conversation, whereas girls stress ability to get along with people. Adolescent boys avoid dates who sulk or pout, act like golddiggers, or are self-centered or fickle. Girls shun boys who are vulgar, conceited, or dilatory in asking for dates.

Compared with other cultures, American culture tends to be rather restrictive about sexual expression among children and adolescents. Nevertheless, according to Kinsey's survey of sexual behavior, many American adolescents indulge in sexual experimentation, kissing, necking, and petting being extremely common. Premarital intercourse increases in frequency as adolescence progresses. In general, adolescent girls engage in considerably less sexual behavior than boys. By the age of 20, about 75 per cent of males, but only 40 per cent of females, have had sexual intercourse.

Standards of acceptable sexual behavior vary with social class. Masturbation is more tolerated and widely practiced among upper- and middle-class boys, whereas intercourse is much more frequent among adolescents of lower class. By age 15, nearly half of lower-class boys, but only 10 per cent of the upper class and middle class, have had sexual intercourse.

Adolescent Attitudes toward Parental Authority. As we have seen, adolescents generally adopt—and peer groups reinforce—their parents' basic moral values. Nevertheless, parent-child conflicts about *specific* rules and about personal goals and values are not uncommon, many of them stemming from the adolescents' strong strivings for independence. According to the data of an extensive survey in Michigan, three-quarters of adolescent girls wish that their parents were less restrictive, particularly with respect to dating. In spite of this discontent, half of the girls considered parental rules beneficial, and only a very small proportion said they were harmful.

Contrary to popular opinion, adolescents do *not* generally regard their parents as traditional or authoritative. In fact, they often see parents as permissive and genuinely concerned with the adolescent's welfare. Most adolescents value and seek parental guidance and protection, and many feel that they would run wild if it were not for parental rules and restrictions. Rebelliousness does not increase with age during adolescence, according to the data of extensive surveys.

Adolescent Values and Beliefs. Many high school students' values and opinions on the relative importance of scholastic achievement and popularity differ from those of their parents. One survey showed, for instance, that over 70 per cent of high school students believe that the chief thing to be learned in school is "how to get along with others," whereas only 14 per cent consider academic learning most important. Most adolescents (approximately 70 per cent) would like to be regarded, or remembered, as "athletic star," "leader," or "most popular" in school; only 30 per cent want to be perceived as "brilliant students." These findings undoubtedly reflect the fact that many adolescents accept the peer group's value system in which high status is associated with popularity, leadership, and athletic attainments, but attach relatively little prestige to intellectual attainments. In contrast to their high school children, most parents—particularly those of the middle class—would prefer to have their children remembered as brilliant students rather than as athletes or social leaders.

There is widespread belief that adolescence is a period of moral confusion, political radicalism, changing values, religious conversions, or disavowal of religion. No doubt the moral and religious attitudes of some adolescents do undergo radical changes. But the vast majority of adolescents espouse the religion of their parents and most maintain attitudes and opinions similar to their parents' in matters of political philosophy and sexual morality. For example, 84 per cent of adolescents are church members, over half attending services regularly, and less than 10 per cent "never or practically never" attend. Although about half express some dissatisfaction with religion, three-quarters have a "firm belief" in God.

Religious beliefs generally become more tolerant and liberal with advancing age, the greatest liberalization occurring between the ages of 12 and 15. During that period, there are significant *increases* with age in the proportion of adolescents agreeing with statements such as "It is not necessary to attend church to be a Christian," and "Catholics, Protestants and Jews are equally good." Fundamentalist beliefs of high school students weaken during the same period, as is attested by the *decreases* with age in the proportion agreeing with statements like "Every word of the Bible is true," and "God watches and punishes wrongdoers."

In spite of the enormous prestige of science and scientists today, science does not seem to be replacing religion in adolescents' value systems. Although, as we have seen, most adolescents maintain their religious beliefs and go to church, many view science and scientists with some suspicion. A surprisingly high percentage of high school students, especially those from poorly educated families, agree that "There is something evil about scientists," and that "Scientists are willing to sacrifice the welfare of others to further their own interests."

ATTITUDES TOWARD MINORITY GROUPS

One of the major social contradictions of American culture involves adherence to democratic principles, on the one hand, and, for many, racial or religious prejudices, on the other. Negative attitudes toward minority groups may develop very early in life. Racial discriminations are fairly well established, at least in some parts of the country, by the age of four. When selecting friends, elementary school children in integrated schools prefer members of their own racial group. White children may manifest anti-Negro prejudices as early as kindergarten and prejudice tends to increase with age, becoming more highly crystallized and conforming more closely to adult patterns. In one study, children between five and eight years of age told stories about pictures depicting minority groups (for example, Negroes and white boys playing; Jewish boys coming out of a synagogue). Many of the youngest revealed prejudices and, with advancing age, the proportion expressing negative attitudes and awareness of intergroup tensions increased.

Children's prejudices are *not* generally based on their own experiences. Group stereotypes and bigotry appear to be reproductions of adult attitudes, learned as a result of direct or indirect teaching, and they may develop in spite of friendly relations between Negro and white children or between Jews and Gentiles. Of course, many children resist bigotry and remain relatively free of prejudice, even if it is prevalent in their culture.

Antecedents of Prejudice

A child may acquire prejudice through identification with intolerant and bigoted parents and the consequent assimilation of their attitudes. In other cases, prejudiced attitudes seem to be an expression of profound feelings of general hostility, which are related to parent-child relationships and to personality structure. Mothers of prejudiced, intolerant children are inclined to be highly critical, rigid, authoritarian, and controlling in their disciplinary practices. By contrast, mothers of unprejudiced children tend to be more permissive, affectionate, and wise in handling their children. In discussing their parents, tolerant youngsters frequently mention affection, cooperation, and companionship, whereas young bigots describe their parents as lacking in affection, stern, harsh, and punitive. As might be anticipated, therefore, prejudiced children have more narrow and rigid personalities, tend to think categorically in terms of "good and bad" or "strong and weak" and are intolerant of anything ambiguous or noncomforming such as passive or feminine behavior in boys and tomboyishness in girls. They tend to accept uncritically the approved values of the groups they identify with.

Prejudiced children are basically frightened and frustrated; superficially they conform to authority, but they harbor deep-seated feelings of hostility and destructiveness. They admire all that is strong, tough, and powerful, but fear weakness in themselves. Characteristically, a prejudiced child lacks confidence in himself; is distrustful, uneasy, and insecure in social relationships; feels discontented about his current status; and is hostile and bitter in his view of the world. When he feels frustrated, as he often does, he blames others, turning his aggression outward, displacing it onto minority groups (prejudice against them being acceptable in the culture), because he fears that other kinds of hostile expression will bring punishment.

Modification of Prejudice

How can prejudices be reduced or eliminated? Many schools in the South of the United States are currently trying to desegregate, or integrate, schools that were previously racially segregated. Will interracial schools decrease anti-Negro prejudice? Unfortunately, definitive answers to these problems are not yet available, but two studies of modifications in children's prejudices in racially integrated settings seem relevant.

The first study was designed to determine whether prejudice would diminish as a result of intimate contact with members of a minority group, and whether such changes (if they occurred) were related to personality characteristics. The subjects, over 100 white New York City boys between eight and fourteen years of age, took tests of racial attitude before and after a four-week vacation at a camp where Negroes and whites lived, ate, and played together. The white boys' personality structures were evaluated by means of personality tests and interviews.

After the camp experience, many children changed their attitudes, some becoming more prejudiced, others more tolerant. According to the personality tests, boys who became more prejudiced had strong underlying hostile feelings and strong needs to defy authority. They perceived the world as cruel, unpleasant, and exploitative, and they felt victimized by others. Yet they could not express their aggressive feelings, since this was likely to bring punishment, retaliation, or restraint. Hence, they displaced their aggressions to the Negroes, against whom they were already prejudiced.

Boys who decreased in prejudice presented different personalities: relatively little feeling of being victimized, less pronounced aggressive needs, and generally favorable attitudes toward others. Moreover, they were happier, better accepted by the other campers, and had more satisfying relationships than those who increased in prejudice. In short, they were better adjusted socially in the interracial situation, identified with it and its equalitarian philosophy, and, consequently, accepted the prevailing unprejudiced attitudes.

We may conclude that intimate contact with minority groups will not, by itself, produce a reduction in prejudice. A child who *needs* to be prejudiced in order to express his own hostility will maintain, or even increase, his prejudices after living with a minority group. Those who do not have such strong aggressive needs, however, are likely to enjoy an interracial experience and may become less prejudiced.

In another recent study, children from low-income families in Southern states attended an interracial camp where they were assigned to integrated cabins. The authority of the counselors supported the rules of the game prescribing equal status and participation for all in all activities. Two weeks of living together in an integrated setting produced no major shifts in long-standing racial attitudes, but the youngsters made significant adjustments rapidly. Judging from their overt behavior, the children accepted, and conformed with, the equalitarian philosophy of the camp, playing and working together happily and with little friction. When asked to name their best friends in their cabins, white children tended to select other whites, but this tendency decreased significantly by the end of the camp period. In general, the children enjoyed the interracial experience, over 75 per cent of them expressing the wish that the camp period could be extended. The investigators felt that the consistent expectation of equality—conveyed by a racially integrated adult culture (the counselors) and expressed in the leaders' unprejudiced behavior—set the tone of the camp and thus produced positive results. Given a favorable situation, attitudes and prejudices may begin to change, even within a brief time span. Nevertheless, the investigators caution that this experience of integration "should probably be viewed not as completing the process of change in intergroup relations but as providing the necessary first steps in a long-term process of reorganizing beliefs and feelings." *

JUVENILE DELINQUENCY

Many cases of juvenile delinquency may reflect failure in socialization—that is, failure to adopt socially acceptable responses, or the moral and ethical standards of the culture. But this is not always true, for, in some subcultural groups, delinquent behavior is accepted or even encouraged. For example, in many metropolitan slum areas, gang warfare and theft may be traditional and approved. Children from such areas may learn these modes of behavior, which are generally considered delinquencies, from their peers. In fact, the vast majority of juvenile delinquents come from poor families living in deteriorating, economically deprived neighborhoods, usually adjacent to the center of a city.

* Yarrow, M. R., Campbell, J. D., and Yarrow, L. F. Interpersonal dynamics in racial integration. In Maccoby, E. E., Newcomb, T. M., and Hartley, Eugene L. (eds.). *Readings in social psychology*. New York: Holt, Rinehart and Winston, 1958, p. 635.

Yet, only a fraction of all impoverished children living in slums actually become delinquent. Obviously, then, socioeconomic factors are not the only significant antecedents of delinquency. Personal insecurities and psychological problems stemming from disturbed family relationships also loom large in the delinquents' backgrounds.

In one classic study, the personalities, attitudes, and social behavior of delinquents were compared with those of their own brothers and sisters who were not delinquents. Of the two groups, more of the former were emotionally unstable, manifested symptoms of neuroses, anxiety and tension, and suffered from profound feelings of inadequacy and inferiority.

The most striking differences between the delinquents and their siblings involved their family relationships, however. An overwhelming percentage (over 90) of the delinquents, but only a few of the nondeliquents, were extremely discontented at home and disturbed because of upsetting experiences with their families. Most of them felt rejected by their parents, deprived, insecure, jealous of their siblings, uncomfortable about family tensions and parental misconduct, or thwarted in their needs for independence or self-expression.

Parents of delinquents are typically lax or erratic in disciplining their children, swinging from overstrictness to overpermissiveness without any consistency. They use physical punishment and ridicule as disciplinary techniques more commonly than other parents do, but seldom employ reasoning and example. In general, the parents of delinquents are considerably less affectionate, warm, or sympathetic—and more indifferent and hostile—toward their children than other parents are. Hence, a delinquent cannot identify readily with his parents and, consequently, he may fail to acquire patterns of acceptable social behavior. Cold, hostile, tense relationships with his parents seem to predispose a child to delinquency, as well as to other forms of maladaptive behavior.

It follows that juvenile delinquency cannot be eliminated, or significantly reduced, exclusively by means of economic welfare programs. Social and psychological facilities must also be available to delinquents (and potential delinquents) to enable them to handle their personal problems more adequately. Most importantly, the need is urgent for psychological, social welfare, and educational programs to aid parents in establishing better relationships with their children.

EPILOGUE

It seems appropriate, for several reasons, to end this volume with discussions of minority group prejudice and delinquency. First of all, although these are *social* problems of vast significance, we must interpret their origins and growth in terms of *psychological development*. That is, these problems are related to personality structure, which is determined, as we have seen repeatedly, by a host of interacting variables—biological, social, and situational. More specifically, we may regard them as the outcomes of certain kinds of social learning and socialization experiences that motivate some *individuals* to behave in ways detrimental to the welfare and happiness of others. Secondly, our discussions sounded an optimistic note: children's socially undesirable behavior and characteristics, like their personal maladjustments, do not develop inevitably and, if they develop, are not necessarily fixed and immutable. Maladjustment, prejudice, and delinquency consist of *acquired,* not biologically determined, patterns of responses and hence are potentially avoidable or modifiable.

For many social and historical reasons, a significant proportion of the research efforts in the young field of child psychology has been focused on socially undesirable behavior and maladjustment. The contributions made to our knowledge of the psychological roots of these problems—contributions having implications for eliminating or ameliorating them—have been substantial. But further, the accumulated knowledge, research techniques, and insights of child psychology may be fruitful in dealing with the other side of the coin. At least in theory, child psychology has the potential for discovering the kinds of social learning experiences that lead to the development of positive characteristics such as personal happiness, emotional maturity, creativity, social tolerance, altruism, humanitarian values, and motivation to contribute to the general welfare. Although few relevant studies have been completed, these problems are the central interests of many outstanding current research programs. For child psychology, the systematic study of the acquisition of behavior and characteristics that promote human welfare and progress seems to be the wave of the future.

Selected Readings

Baldwin, A. L. *Behavior and development in childhood.* New York: Holt, Rinehart and Winston (Dryden), 1955.

Carmichael, L. (Ed.). *Manual of child psychology.* New York: Wiley, 1954.

Elkin, F. *The child and society.* New York: Random House, 1960.

Erikson, E. The course of healthy personality development. Midcentury White House Conference on Children and Youth. In Seidman, J. M. (Ed.). *The adolescent—a book of readings.* New York: Holt, Rinehart and Winston, 1960.

Gesell, A., and Ilg, F. L. *Child development.* New York: Harper & Row, 1949.

Goodenough, F. L., and Tyler, L. E. *Developmental psychology.* New York: Appleton-Century-Crofts, 1959.

Hunt, J. McV. *Intelligence and experience.* New York: Ronald, 1961.

Kuhlen, R. G. *The psychology of adolescent development.* New York: Harper, 1952.

McCandless, B. R. *Children and adolescents—behavior and development.* New York: Holt, Rinehart and Winston, 1961.

Miller, D. R., and Swanson, G. E. *Inner conflict and defense.* New York: Holt, Rinehart and Winston, 1960.

Mussen, P. H. (Ed.). *Handbook of research methods in child development.* New York: Wiley, 1960.

Mussen, P. H., Conger, J. J., and Kagan, J. *Child development and personality.* New York: Harper & Row, 1963.

Sears, R. R., Maccoby, E. E., and Levin, H. *Patterns of child rearing.* New York: Harper & Row, 1957.

Stone, L. J., and Church, J. *Childhood and adolescence.* New York: Random House, 1957.

Tanner, J. M. *Growth at adolescence.* Springfield, Ill.: Charles C. Thomas Publisher, 1955.

Wallace, A. F. C. *Culture and personality.* New York: Random House, 1961.

Whiting, J. W. M., and Child, I. L. *Child training and personality.* New Haven: Yale University Press, 1953.

Index

Index

A

B

C

D

E

F

G

N

O

P

R